WHO'S THIS
SITTING IN MY PEW?

Faith Bowers was born in Croydon and grew up in Stroud, Gloucestershire. She and her family, including her son Richard who features prominently in this book, now live in South London, and are members of Bloomsbury Central Baptist Church. She is a member of the Council of the Baptist Union and a Baptist representative on the British Council of Churches. Since 1983 she has convened the Baptist Union working group on mental handicap and the Church, which produced under her editorship a resource book, *Let Love be Genuine*; and she also serves on the committee of CHAD – Church Action on Disability.

Faith Bowers

Who's This Sitting in My Pew?

MENTALLY HANDICAPPED PEOPLE IN THE CHURCH

TRi△NGLE

First published 1988
Triangle/SPCK
Holy Trinity Church
Marylebone Road
London NW1 4DU

Copyright © Faith Bowers 1988

British Library Cataloguing in Publication Data

Bowers, Faith
    Who's this sitting in my pew ? : mentally
    handicapped people in the church.
    1. Handicapped — Religious life
    I. Title
    248.8′6   BV4910

    ISBN 0-281-04340-X

Typeset by Inforum Ltd, Portsmouth
Printed and bound in Great Britain by
Hazell Watson & Viney Limited
Member of BPCC plc
Aylesbury Bucks

For
RICHARD

Acknowledgements

The handicapped people who appear in this book are real, although most names have been changed. I am grateful to the many friends who have shared their stories with me in the hope that others will understand that these are indeed real people.

I am especially grateful to Brian Astill, Joyce Beak, Eileen Bebbington, David Clark, Barbara Crowe, Trisha Dale, Margaret Griffiths, Judy Martin, and Susan Wright for multiple contributions, and to Ernest Bladon and Audrey Saunders who each collected material from others as well as relating their own experience. Some forty others also supplied me with items, but most would not want themselves, and hence their handicapped friends, identified.

Above all I thank my son, Richard, who has provided the incentive and so much of the content for this book. Without his help it could not have been written and he will enjoy finding his own name recurring within.

FAITH BOWERS
August 1987

Contents

1
The Changing Face of Mental Handicap

'Dear Keith, I am a college student too,' wrote Richard with satisfaction to his brother away at university. He had just begun a further education course at a technical college a few miles from home.

Richard is mentally handicapped, with the common genetic defect known as Down's Syndrome. It amazes us, his parents, to see how educable he is still proving in spite of severe limitations. The very fact that he can write a short letter is beyond our boldest hopes of ten years ago. Writing is still quite taxing and he usually prefers to use the telephone, while after Christmas, faced with the need to write a number of similar 'thank you' letters, he asked if he could borrow Dad's computer. He had it all worked out for maximum economy of effort too. All letters beginning 'Dear Auntie —' should be done in succession, so that only the Christian name and gift needed changing!

The college course is designed primarily to increase the degree of independence such students achieve. Richard travels there alone, two trains each way. The protected child, transported for years door-to-door between home and school, suddenly grew up into a London commuter. He did so with remarkably little trouble, taking great delight in this daily achievement. The railway staff keep a kindly eye open for him, and they tell me they have enjoyed watching his confidence and competence increase.

Richard was born in 1969, just before the Education (Handicapped Children) Act of 1970 decreed that education should be provided for children with severe mental handicaps, 'the last to come in' to the education system. Special schools, with properly qualified teachers, replaced the Junior Training Centres.

By the time Richard reached school age, education was

1

established as a right. It meant a lot to us, his parents, to see him settling into an infants' class and school routine recognisably similar to his brother's, even if the pace was slower. The most obvious difference was the small class size.

The achievements of these schools have gradually shown that some may benefit from appropriate further education and suitable courses are being developed. So Richard has progressed from schoolboy to student.

The goals for achievement offered us by consultants when Richard was new-born were that in time he would probably learn to wash, dress and feed himself. 'Would he be able to *think* at all?' I asked, but that apparently was not a proper question. The doctor did not attempt to answer. I assume that he did not mean to be unduly depressing, but even so recently a paediatrician had little idea of how much could be achieved by many with Down's Syndrome.

What image is conjured up in your mind by the mention of mental handicap?

That will vary according to your experience, but most people have had no close, personal contact with a mentally handicapped person. Perhaps your picture is of someone pathetic, with poor control over his body and very limited awareness of life around him. Sadly some are like that, but the range of mental handicap is wide. Many people, in spite of severe limitations, can lead remarkably full lives.

With changing provision for their needs, we can in future expect to see many more handicapped people around, taking part in the normal life of society in ways that may surprise us.

A neighbour of mine was told that her son, with a rare condition, would never sit up or speak. I saw her the other day, giving him a hand down the steps of the school bus. He chatted to her about his day as they walked up the road. His gait is awkward, his speech limited, but he is far more *alive* than anyone expected. His mother laughed with me about the problems she had never dared hope for: like having her eleven-year-old clean the bath with toothpaste applied on his brother's new vest. She knows I understand, but I realise how lightly I get off with Richard – mostly!

A new generation of mentally handicapped youth is now emerging from school. For them the change from training to teaching has meant raised expectations and greater achievement. Parents today receive more help and guidance in the early stimulation of handicapped babies. In schools skilled teachers continue to stretch the children's minds. They are not more intelligent, but more are being enabled to realise their full potential.

Community care

Not only in education have state policies changed dramatically. Families are no longer encouraged to place severely handicapped children in special hospitals, often far from their homes. A century ago such institutions were a humane provision and Christians were well to the fore in establishing Idiot Asylums. Many of their successors, the subnormality hospitals, have been good, providing a safe and pleasant environment. Others have not done so well and when the poor conditions in some hit the headlines a few years ago there was a public outcry.

It is now government policy not to place children in such hospitals, but to provide places in smaller units for those who cannot remain at home. Further, people already in large and often remote institutions, where some have lived for many years, are being moved out into smaller homes and hostels. This process is proceeding briskly. One Kent hospital, for example, had over 1000 residents until recently. By the end of 1986 only 550 were left and the hospital is due to close in 1994. This pattern is being repeated at present all over the country. The first people to emerge will be those who are relatively able. We may wonder why they were ever shut away. Even so, after years out of society, the transition will be traumatic for many. As the process proceeds to the less able, it is not going to get easier.

Community care is an enlightened policy, but it too has its problems, especially in these transition years when changes are being made with good intent and limited resources. It

3

makes new demands on society at large but, handled well, the new patterns of care can change lives for the better, even for adults who have been long 'institutionalised'.

Tom had lived in hospital for seventeen years. Three years ago he was referred to a Community Living Project. The nursing staff felt that his 'severe behavioural outbursts' were due to his environment and believed he was capable of learning to lead a new life. He had never had any formal education and was quite anxious about leaving the hospital.

With three others, Tom moved to a staffed house, first on the edge of the hospital grounds and then in a permanent home in the town. He has learnt many new skills – cooking, cleaning, doing his own laundry, paying bills and crossing the road. He now works one day a week at a local garden centre and his boss would like him to increase this to two.

Since leaving hospital, Tom's ability and skills have developed so greatly that it now seems possible to think of him living with less staff support and earning his own living. Tom's father summed it up: 'Now I can say I am proud of my son. I never thought this would be possible.'

Members of the local community

We shall probably continue to see little of those who are profoundly, often multiply, handicapped. They will continue to be known only to those who care for them and perhaps to a few other friends who go out of their way to help.

Other mentally handicapped people – some only a bit 'slower' than is deemed 'normal', others severely affected and the whole range in between – will be seen around more in future. They will use the shops and public transport, even the public library; they may serve us in the café or supermarket; they may become regulars at the local pub; and they may come to our local church.

Will we welcome these new neighbours? Will we be ready with help and encouragement when it is needed? Will we stare after them with curiosity or turn away with embarrassment? Will we accept them as part of the community?

We may all need to look again and adjust our ideas about people with mental handicaps. It is hard to generalise: they are all individuals. Yet they are not so different from the rest of us. They share many of our basic needs, feelings and pleasures.

Many can certainly think. They may have good memories and be capable of putting two and two together. Most cannot cope with abstract concepts and their thought processes may be slow, but they can think about things that are within their experience. Many can learn to do a variety of things well, but the learning process may be prolonged.

If other people allow for this, there is a better chance of mentally handicapped people fitting into the community and leading richer lives; people like George, Brenda and Terry, who have all taken part in a resettlement programme.

George had lived in hospital from the age of fourteen to fifty-eight. He had occasional aggressive outbursts, but was generally sociable and well liked. He was very anxious to leave hospital to live with a family, and also to regain contact with his sister. He settled into his carer family extremely well, loving the three small children with whom he was unfailingly gentle. He made many friends at a social club. George was so happy that he referred his handicapped brother to the project. They want to be in contact but not live together. Their sister visits regularly.

Brenda went to the hospital when her father died and her mother had to go to work to keep the family. She was eleven. Losing all family contact, she grew up to be very possessive, and constantly stole food and money from other residents in the hospital. She was fifty-five when she left the hospital to live with a carer. There have been no stealing incidents whatever since. At first she was jealous if her carer spoke to other people, which was understandable. As Brenda became more secure, her relationships became more normal. She learned many domestic skills and, six months after leaving the hospital, joined an art class.

Terry lived in hospital for thirty-one years. A cheerful, sociable character, his speech is not clear but his smile tells a lot. Terry moved into a staffed house and quickly became chief tea-maker for the other residents. He was always full of fun, but it became obvious that he had no family or friends of his own beyond the hospital and project. He was referred to the project's People-to-People programme, who recruited and trained a family who would like to take Terry into their own home. When he gets to know them better, he will decide whether he wants to live with this family or remain with his friends in the staffed house. For the first time in his life, Terry will have a real choice of where to live.

The churches, centres of love and care within society, ought to be alert to the needs of mentally handicapped people like these. Christians do not doubt that Jesus loves the handicapped. We must not assume too readily that there are none in our neighbourhood. There probably are, and it is to them that we could be instruments of Christian love.

2
The Challenge to the Church

Richard had gone swimming with his cousins. The pool was not one of their regular haunts. After twenty minutes racing, retrieving underwater and the like, they had paused for a chat when the attendants changed over. The new one took one look at Richard, doubtless thought 'What's a mongol doing here?' and told him he must stay below the shallow water marker.

She did not enquire whether he could swim, nor did she impose any restriction on his younger cousin, a diminutive boy, often taken for much less than his twelve years. It might have been fair enough to ask Richard to demonstrate his prowess, but she just assumed incompetence and so spoiled the session for them all.

In fact Richard has swum enthusiastically since early childhood and has quite a powerful crawl, even if too splashy for good style.

Happily we have not often encountered such attitudes towards Richard but there is still plenty of prejudice around, presenting additional problems for handicapped people trying to live 'out in the community'.

Christians are not immune to prejudice and preconceived ideas, and they too are quite capable of imposing unnecessary restrictions because they do not bother to find out what the individual can do.

Influencing public opinion

For many years few people with severe mental handicaps were seen around in society. Here and there one lived at home and was known in the immediate neighbourhood, but the majority were cared for in special establishments, usually away from centres of population. The move to community

7

care changes that. More are seen: they are not always welcome.

In the more distant past, the 'village idiot' was familiar enough, tolerated, teased by the children, but often finding a useful role within the local community. He is often encountered in books. In *Waverley* (published in 1814) Sir Walter Scott describes such a man, kindly treated by Baron Bradwardine whom he served usefully in spite of his bizarre behaviour.

> David Gellatly was in good earnest the half-crazed simpleton which he appeared, and was incapable of any constant and steady exertion. He had just so much solidity as kept on the windy side of insanity; so much wild wit as saved him from the imputation of idiocy; some dexterity in field sports; great kindness and humanity in the treatment of animals intrusted to him; warm affections, a prodigious memory, and an ear for music.

Community care worked well for David Gellatly, as it can for many in real life today once society has learned to tolerate their peculiarities and appreciate their gifts.

Confusion with mental illness

Scott describes David as a 'half-crazed simpleton': there is too often confusion between mental handicap and mental illness. Although both can occur in one person, they are different and do not usually go together. A physical analogy may be helpful: blindness is a physical handicap, pneumonia is a physical illness. Our response to the two sufferers is quite different. Yet people persist in muddling mental handicap and mental illness, which is not helpful to those afflicted with either. This popular misunderstanding affects even those who might be expected to know better, including too many clergy.

The confusion between mental handicap and illness is increased because community care policies are currently being applied to both. An article in my local paper last year told sympathetically of a project to establish a group home for three mentally handicapped adults. As part of an appeal for funds the writer observed, truly but irrelevantly, that 'none

8

of us can be sure that a member of our family or a much-loved friend will not suffer from mental illness'.

As a rough definition, *mental illness* may afflict anyone, however intelligent, and being an illness it may be susceptible to treatment and can often be cured. *Mental handicap* implies that the brain is fundamentally limited and not capable of full 'normal' development. There may be various reasons for this, including genetic abnormalities, physical damage at birth or from a later accident, damage from biochemical disorders or as a result of certain diseases. Such damage cannot be cured, the handicap is there for good: all that can be done is to help the person to develop as fully as he or she is able.

There are conditions where the boundary lines are not so clear cut. Autism, for example, is a handicapping condition with severe psychological disturbance. Other mental handicaps may give rise to weird behaviour, more than 'half-crazed', but generally mental illness and mental handicap are distinct and different.

Peculiar logic

Many mentally handicapped people are pleasant and well-balanced; their minds work calmly and logically, even if we find the process slow and the logic hard to follow, based as it must be upon their limited experience and understanding.

Sometimes we as parents still have great difficulty in grasping what Richard is talking about, not because of his imperfect diction but rather because we just do not follow the way his mind works. When we get there, we can in retrospect see the connections, so obvious to him that he does not attempt to spell them out.

Part of the difficulty is that Richard has an excellent memory but a rather hazy idea of time past. He may see a climbable-looking tree and go off into a rigmarole, punctuated with '*You* remember, Mum'. Is the memory of his cousin hiding in a tree last holidays, or of his aunt amusing the children by her monkey antics some years ago, or of hearing the story of Zacchaeus in Sunday School?

9

It is even harder for those who know him less intimately. He has recently made a stamp collection as part of his work for a Duke of Edinburgh Award. The assessor asked him how he set about collecting. 'Well,' said Richard, 'I go to church.' Full stop. The assessor might have wondered whether Richard failed to understand the question – or was he *so* careful to commend each separate activity to God in prayer? Fortunately his father was present and could draw Richard on to explain that several friends at church gather stamps for him and he never leaves on Sunday without some fresh ones for his collection. His answer was true, if barely adequate.

Public fears

Ignorance and misunderstandings breed fear. The word goes round that a charity wants to buy that house down the road for a group of mentally handicapped people and the neighbours are alarmed. Is there a threat to their children's safety? What will it do to house prices in the road? As rumour spreads, it always embroiders and exaggerates.

At this stage a responsible person, perhaps a Christian, may exert a check.

'I can see there might be problems,' says Mrs Owens, over a cup of coffee with her friend, 'but don't you think we should try to find out more about them? There must be someone we could ask. What about your friend who's a district nurse – could she tell us who to contact? Surely the hospital would not be letting them out if they were dangerous sex maniacs or likely to go round damaging property? Perhaps we ought to give them a fair chance.'

Such resettlement must be carefully planned and the social workers responsible would probably like to talk to the neighbours about it. Perhaps a meeting might be arranged by the church on the corner. Mrs Owens and her friend, their sympathy thus enlisted, might visit their prospective neighbours and get to know them so that, as friends, they could help them settle in after the move.

Sadly it does not always happen like that. Residents'

Associations have been known to organise protests with media support, neighbours have arranged to gazump the charity, and newcomers have been made to feel distinctly unwelcome. The more comfortably 'respectable' the area, the harder it may be to gain acceptance. Even when a group has been settled for some time and seems part of the local community, pockets of resentment can survive.

Jack is about thirty. Behind his glasses his eyes have a far-away look, but his appearance and gait are not strikingly odd to suggest his disability to strangers. He attends faithfully every activity of the nearby church, so when he missed the Harvest Supper a church friend called to see if all was well. Jack had been beaten up at four o'clock in the afternoon outside the local shop. No money had been stolen, but some youths had just lashed into him, injuring his face and leaving him badly shaken. They jumped on a bus and got away. The attendant at the home, a tough-looking young man, was almost beside himself with rage that anyone could do such a thing to gentle Jack. It shook the church too. The people there had grown fond of Jack and his friends and had thought they were generally well accepted locally.

Not long afterwards a League of Friends was set up to support the home. The church hall was booked for an inaugural meeting, chaired by the MP. Worthy citizens and social workers were surprised when several residents from the home turned up. Church friends present were quietly pleased. These residents all came regularly to worship and evidently felt confident to come to any meeting on the church premises.

That meeting went well, but even people prepared to put themselves out to help can be cruelly careless in their attitudes. After a meeting of another body, noted for community concerns, which among other things provided transport to a club for mentally handicapped young people, a father was hurt to overhear the remark, 'I'm on the loony trip next Monday'.[1]

Community care presents a challenge to all caring bodies in society, not least the churches, which ought to be aware of schemes for the handicapped in their area and should submit instinctive reactions to scrutiny in the light of Christian values. If there is vocal opposition, the church may need to speak out on behalf of the oppressed.

Describing the condition

Richard's tutor was arranging a week's work experience for some of her students. Over the phone to local firms she explained that they had 'learning difficulties'. When she took Richard for an interview, the personnel officer and manager were visibly dismayed. 'Learning difficulties' had not conveyed to them 'mental handicap' as the Down's features did.

There are real problems over terminology. The professionals working in the field are constantly changing the 'acceptable' terms, for the best of reasons, but it becomes awfully confusing. Words can get outworn and come to carry too weighted a sense. 'Idiot' and 'imbecile' were Victorian classifications, which survived till relatively recently, although everyday usage had long lost the original distinction. 'Cretin', the name originally given to those physically deformed and mentally handicapped by a thyroid deficiency, was actually derived from the French form of 'Christian', stressing the recognition that those afflicted still belonged to the human race. Any word used as a technical description of low intelligence is likely to acquire a more general, pejorative sense. It is a pity the change is now usually from single words to clumsy phrases. I understand why 'my son who has Down's Syndrome' is preferred to 'my mongol son', but it is a mouthful. At present 'special needs', 'severe learning difficulties' and 'intellectual impairment' are in, and professionals have to use approved terms.

Parents, perhaps more aware of lay understanding, are often less happy to use euphemisms which conceal the painful truth unless the hearers know them as current technical terms. As I see it, our friend's dyslexic son, who did not learn to read till he was ten but now has an honours degree, had severe learning difficulties – but in quite a different way from Richard!

For this reason, and although I know some will disapprove, I have generally used the term *mentally handicapped*, which everybody understands and which is clear and honest but has no particularly unkind connotations.

Terms matter less than attitudes.

Recently I dropped Richard off at the youth club, where he is the only handicapped member, and watched him joking with one of the girls. Something he said evoked a friendly shove and the laughing response, 'You are an idiot, Richard!'

That she could so address him, just as she might any of the others, spoke volumes about the integration achieved there.

What are they really like?

When Maisie Owens and Jill Dean set out for the hospital to meet their prospective neighbours, they did not really know what to expect. It was a bit frightening. If they found it all too awful, would they be able to hide their revulsion? Would conversation be possible? By the time they reached the hospital gates, they were tempted to turn the car round and escape.

Tess, the social worker, met them and took them first to a room which seemed to be full of queer-looking people, some slumped in wheelchairs, many with oddly proportioned bodies. Some chorused a greeting and asked, 'Who are you? Who are you?' Others ignored them. Jim was sitting down, watching television. Peter and Bill proved to be the two playing snooker at the far end of the room and were in no hurry to abandon their game.

Jill and Maisie were relieved to withdraw to a smaller room with Tess and the three young men who were to be their neighbours. Tess had explained that the three were friends and were receiving careful training to look after themselves.

Peter was quite tall, with abundant fair hair. He was almost good-looking but there was something oddly distorted about the set of his eyes, as though his forehead had been twisted. He had a quiet, gentle manner, understood what was said to him, and could answer sensibly but slowly. It seemed as though his mind knew what to say but had difficulty in transmitting thoughts into speech. Articulation required a great effort, although the words came out clearly at the end.

Bill was short and dark, with the distinctive features and stumpy, awkward fingers of Down's Syndrome. His speech was less clear than Peter's and tended to come in a jerky rush, although he would cheerfully repeat phrases more slowly and carefully if asked. At first Maisie and Jill found him very hard to follow, but gradually they began to 'tune in' to him and caught more words. He was cheerful and enthusiastic about the new home, and told them he was looking forward to growing things in the garden, pretty flowers, tomatoes and beans. 'And lettuces?' suggested Jill. 'No,' said Bill. 'Don't like lettuce. Like cats. You got cat?' Maisie had and promised he could come and see it.

Jim was short and square, the proportions of his body all awry. His limbs worked clumsily and his head projected awkwardly from his shoulders, almost without neck, its movement restricted. Surprisingly, his face looked normal, the expression bright and pleasant. He was friendly and curious and asked lots of questions but did not seem good at remembering the answers, for he would ask the same thing again a little later. 'Have you got a house? Is it a big house? Do you have your own room? I'm going to have my own bedroom, just for me. Have you got a garden? Have you got a dog? We've got to wash our own clothes. Bill's a good cook. Have you got a garden?' and so on.

'Well, that wasn't so bad after all', said Jill as they drove home. 'In one way they're pathetic, yet they seem happy and friendly. I must see if I can get some plants together to help Bill start his garden off. I'm sure I'll have plenty to spare'.

'They'll miss the snooker table', mused Maisie. 'I wonder if my boys would mind them using ours sometimes – they appeared to play quite well. I wonder if they'd like to come to church?'

So often people imagine they know what handicapped people are like without bothering to find out. Professionals, as well as society at large, too easily think in stereotypes and even kindly preconceptions get in the way of seeing the individual himself. He has Down's Syndrome therefore he is affectionate, musical, placid . . . They are not all like that. Parents and teachers are often more inclined to think their one common feature is obstinacy. Even if the generalisations are true, who wants to have all their nicer characteristics written off as merely part of their condition?

What is certain is that having known one mentally handicapped person does not mean that you know them all. They are all different, just as school teachers or shop assistants are not all alike. You have to meet each one with an open mind and find out what he or she is really like. Christians understand that God values each person individually; that understanding ought to challenge the tendency to stereotype the handicapped.

Another temptation is to see them as children, as Peter Pans who will never grow up. In some ways they may remain childlike and people who are at ease with children may find themselves good at talking to mentally handicapped adults. Yet they are grown up and their experience and feelings are not those of a child. Many of them are well aware that people treat them like children and they do not like it.

Professional help

The movement to community care involves careful preparation and ongoing support. A variety of professions will be involved: social workers, community nurses, psychologists, therapists, and so on. Some homes will have resident staff, others will be regularly visited to ensure that the more independent are coping. There still remains a lot that can be done, indeed, can often only be done, by friendly neighbours. It is an area where the professional staff will welcome support from well-disposed local people, so it is worth approaching such staff for information and guidance to direct kind efforts into the most helpful channels.

Churches wanting to welcome these newcomers should find the hospital chaplain particularly helpful. The chaplaincy service has built up expertise over the years and, in their concern for people being returned to the community beyond the hospital, chaplains will be glad to advise.

All these professional people have the interests of those being resettled at heart, so they will be open to approaches from individuals or community groups seeking better information to allay fears or wanting to make them welcome.

Just being friendly

Information about support arrangements and about individual abilities, interests and particular difficulties all help, but being good neighbours really comes down to being friendly. How do you express friendliness to your other neighbours? That is probably the best way to begin.

Have a chat over the gate, grouse about the weather, mention anything interesting that is going on locally. Do you ask neighbours in for coffee? The handicapped will not have a car: would they, like many elderly folk, love to be invited out for a country drive?

These new friends may be hospitable themselves and quite capable of having neighbours in to tea. Would you hesitate to accept an invitation?

A few years ago I heard a young, blind mother talking on the radio. She spoke calmly, sympathetically even, of 'the fear sighted mothers have of us – and I really think it is fear'. She found, for example, that after meeting their children from school local mothers often had a cup of tea in one or other home. The invitation would include the blind mother and her child but when she asked the others to her house they made excuses. She supposed they were embarrassed because they could not imagine how she could cope.

If mentally handicapped people are living independent or semi-independent lives, they will be capable of serving tea. Sometimes it may be more blessed to receive!

Fully themselves as they are

We live in an age that expects cures. The great strides in

16

medicine in this century leave us less ready than earlier generations to accept, especially where children are concerned, that things wrong cannot be put right. Parents used to accept in sorrow that many children died early in life from diseases that are rarely life-threatening in the West today. Victorian literature is full of such tragedies bravely borne. Nowadays we are less ready to resign ourselves to the 'inevitable'. This adds to the difficulty of accepting that a child has a condition that cannot be cured. In mental handicap the brain has not developed normally, or has been damaged, and that is a state that has to be lived with.

In the early years as parents we found people kept asking – and praying – that Richard should be 'healed' or 'made whole'. It was one of the hardest things, trying to explain patiently to kind friends and relations that it was no good humping the baby round to specialists or healers, he was as he was, the genetic abnormality was a part of him through and through.

The emphasis on healing miracles, always within the church but particularly strong in recent years, does not always help those coming to terms with handicap. To some 'healing' will only be granted in a spiritual way, as we learn acceptance. That may be a significant psychological development but is not what most have in mind when looking for miracles.

In the first weeks of Richard's life, when the handicapping condition was suggested but not certain, we were not alone in our desperate prayers that he should be found – or made – normal. Confirmation that he had Down's Syndrome was devastating. At that stage it was important for the survival of our faith that we accepted the facts. Only then could we begin to come to terms with the child we had and set about doing our best for him, strengthened by the belief that in God's love good could come from what seemed to us pretty bad.

Those first three weeks of Richard's life were strange. Usually Down's Syndrome is diagnosed at once, although many other mental handicaps only become apparent gradually, as the baby fails to develop at the expected pace. For us

17

there was this period of 'suspended animation', when we went about the daily routine of caring for a sweetly helpless, newborn baby without feeling able to respond to him emotionally. We would have loved a normal child. Once we knew he was handicapped, we could relate to him as he was: the love was able to flood in despite our disappointment and anxieties. The prayer changed from 'Let him be all right' to 'Let his life somehow be useful'. The temptation was to feel that the extra effort of rearing a handicapped child was futile, so it was no longer 'healing' we sought but the grace to accept and the hope that there was some point to it all.

The timing sharpened our awareness of this shift in attitude, but it is common to many parents' experience. Some wrestle with why God allows it to happen, some accept the gift of a 'special child', some lose their faith in a loving God, some never had it anyway, some see healing miracles in the progress their child does make; but to make a good job of rearing a child with any handicap the parents have to recognise that that is how their child is. You cannot always be fighting the facts. If the child is blind or deaf, you have to accept the need to work through the other senses. If the child has severe difficulties in learning, you have to recognise that and then search for ways of stimulating and teaching him. Thus one helps them 'realise their full potential'. That process is perhaps a form of 'healing'. Christian friends who grasp this will also recognise that this child, like every other, is precious in God's sight as he or she is.

Their own perceptions

People with physical handicaps speak of the need for others to recognise they are fully themselves as they are, that their personal *wholeness* includes the deaf ears or unresponsive limbs. The fortunate majority, clearly 'whole' in body and mind, do not find this recognition comes naturally. When we see people with severe disabilities as whole people in their own right, we are on the way to treating them with respect and understanding: the relationship is freed to become 'normal'.

18

People with mental handicaps are less likely to talk about their *wholeness* but that does not mean they cannot feel it.

We dreaded the day when Richard would realise he was handicapped. We feared it would come painfully when he reached seventeen and was not allowed to learn to drive. In fact, it came a few months earlier because he was curious about a book Mum was writing. When I explained it was about mentally handicapped people like him, he was indignant: 'Me? Handicapped! How dare you!' Yet as he came to understand more, it was helpful all round. Over driving he was anxious that we recognise his knowledge of the functions of the car controls, but accepted that he thinks too slowly for safe judgement. He contents himself with keen back-seat driving: 'Why did you cross that orange light?' 'Dad, why do you change gear at corners where Keith doesn't?' (The Cortina behaves differently from his brother's Mini).

Eager for increasing independence, he accepts why we practise each new stage before he is trusted alone. He is alert to other handicaps, often calling us to see television items that show disabled people. He thinks it is harder for young people in wheelchairs to make friends than for someone like him, 'because people talk over their heads and leave them out'.

Early this year Richard became aware of election speculation. 'Mum,' he asked suspiciously, 'when I'm eighteen will I get a vote, or not *because I'm mentally handicapped*?' Reassured, he was peeved a few months later when the chosen date was three days short of his birthday! I suppose that next time he will vote with the same mixture of prejudice and intuitive response to television presentations that characterise many voters. He and his friends are not so different from other young people, discussing their reactions to the party leaders in the news, just as they discuss sports heroes and pop singers. They all watch the same programmes after all.

Rising above pity

The normal reaction to mental handicap is fear and revulsion: or is it? We have more often met with sympathy and kindness. Curiosity, yes – and I still catch myself looking twice at someone 'odd'. Out and about with a Down's child much in evidence, we have generally met with a kind response.

And that can be singularly painful. In the early years the tears would prick when total strangers came across to murmur, 'Dear little thing – they're so loving, those children.' Even in the midst of a happy outing, into which the child fitted as easily as his brother, some people could not let you forget. Worst were those who kept on about these delightful children 'bringing their own love with them', 'knowing no evil', 'who will never sin'. Sometimes I had to bite back the commiseration that these consolers were only blessed with able children. I knew they meant well but I wished they could think of something more sensible to say. The clichés of pity can be hard to receive.

Others would admit they did not know what to say and take an interest in what the baby was wearing or the child playing with, or talk about something refreshingly different. They felt inadequate; we felt their sympathy.

It is painful to get alongside those who are suffering in any way. Perhaps the corollary of the second beatitude may be 'Blessed are the comforters, for they take others' pain upon themselves.'

If people try to avoid the mentally handicapped, it may be because they do not know how to treat them. When they realise that a 'normal' response may be appropriate, they are often positively kind and patient. Many shop assistants, faced with a handicapped customer, will handle the transaction calmly and pleasantly, giving him time to make himself understood, helping to sort out the right payment or count out the change. I have had shopkeepers, with no special training to deal with handicapped people, rebuke me for trying to speed Richard up, conscious of the growing queue behind. 'No, let him count the money himself. Now, what is this big one? Yes, ten pence. So add on three – use my fingers too . . .' And these amateur teachers in a real-life situation would command his attention, so lacking in 'sums' lessons at school.

20

Richard and his friends are sharply aware of other people's attitudes to them. On the whole Richard, a cheerful extrovert, shakes off the nastier ones, but occasionally he will mention that someone called him silly names, or deliberately kicked him in passing. He tells us there is nice teasing and nasty teasing, easily distinguished. He has never complained of anyone calling him a 'mongol', but particularly objects to shouts of what he hears as 'Plastic!' It would offend sufferers from cerebral palsy too: they are by no means all of low intelligence yet in popular parlance 'spastic' has recently come to imply that. The disabled have to get used to that kind of attack from the more fortunate. It is part of the price of life in the community.

Challenge to communicate

Speech problems frequently accompany mental handicap – and speech is our dominant means of communication. Some handicapped people have little or no speech, others may be fairly fluent but not articulate clearly, others again have normal speech which in turn can be deceptive.

'Have you talked to Sam? He's really quite bright', people say of a man often at church. If you talk to him regularly, you soon realise that the range of topics on which Sam can talk 'intelligently' is very limited indeed, and the same conversations recur again and again.

This repetition of subjects in which they are fluent is quite common. Rodney came to church when visiting his parents for the monthly weekend. Back at the hostel his room overlooked the backyard, and for several months he treated friends to a detailed description of their refuse disposal and the joys of dustbin day!

Often those with serious speech problems become adept at non-verbal communication. By the time Richard began to talk, he had developed a considerable 'vocabulary' in mime and gesture, to which he still occasionally resorts when we persistently fail to understand. Only once, as a child, was he quick to answer the minister's question in a children's address. The preacher decided to catch youthful attention by miming a key theme and Richard was one of the first to identify it and call out 'fishing'.

When he was fifteen, we went to the European Baptist Federation Congress in Hamburg. It was fascinating to watch Richard. While we experimented with school French and less German to communicate with Finns, Rumanians or Portuguese, Richard made friends with everyone he sat near. He smiled and showed them things and chattered away in English, content with their replies in whatever tongue. One afternoon we went on a different outing from the boys and returned to seek them in the huge auditorium: people from all over Europe could recognise Richard's parents and directed us to where he and his brother were sitting.

It is possible to convey a surprising amount by gesture and facial expression. If we are not too self-conscious to use it, bold and clear, we can meet half-way those who find it hard to understand our speech and to articulate their own.

Handicapped people are generally sensitive to atmosphere and catch the mood when they do not follow the words. So they may be uncomfortably good at differentiating between sincerity and a superficial display of goodwill – tough if you mean well but are ill at ease with them!

Richard enjoys being among people who are happy and laughing, even if he cannot understand the jokes. He just likes the atmosphere. Thus he always enjoyed comedy programmes on television, even if they depended heavily on verbal humour. When we acquired a video-recorder, we were surprised to discover that if these were recorded and he watched them several times he would actually get the jokes, which were not beyond him as we had imagined but just too quick. Having got the idea, he catches some first time round these days. Among other teenagers who make him welcome, he responds to a jolly atmosphere. They can tell him he is daft when he gets things wrong and he will accept it as fair comment and laugh with them. He knows when the words are meant to hurt.

Often schools teach a simple sign language. It is worth

22

finding out whether handicapped friends use this. If so, others at church may well find it worth learning to sign. When Richard's college friends visited our house recently, I found that one, who spoke fluently enough when plying me with questions about our light fittings and how the dimmer switches worked, reverted to signing for basic requests, like a drink. As Richard has not learned a formal sign language, I was painfully slow on the uptake.

Often the handicapped know very well that others have difficulty in understanding them. They are patient about repeating things and inventive at reinforcing unclear words with gesture and mime. It must be terribly frustrating and it is not surprising if some get agitated and resort to tantrums not unlike those typical of toddlers, also at the stage of knowing what they want to get across but unable to put it into words.

Communication – both understanding and making oneself understood – is a real challenge.

Challenge of better education

As outlined in the opening chapter, developments in education for all with serious learning difficulties have brought their own challenge in recent years. Many more young people with mental handicaps are achieving a measure of independence and they value it. Friends need to be aware of what they can do for themselves, and also of the areas where they really need help and, perhaps, protection. It is easy to patronise them and do for them things they can do for themselves and even for others.

A visitor to a church class for severely handicapped young people went to help fold the wheelchairs when those from a local home had been helped back into their minibus. Mike became agitated and stopped her. 'This is my job', he explained, 'it's what I can do for Jesus'.[2]

Those who have learned to read and even (for it is harder) to write, will probably take a pride in these skills and like to use them. In this the handicapped may be rather different

23

from other people who are barely literate and rather ashamed of it. Those competent in other ways but conscious that they read with difficulty will avoid the embarrassing activity where possible, so they do not create much demand for adult literature that is easy to read.

That is partly the reason for the lack of suitable reading material for handicapped adults. This dearth is true of all fields, not least religion. It is a matter of concern to librarians who service adult day centres and find a surprising enthusiasm for books although so few are really appropriate. Publishers feel the market is too small to be commercially viable, which is sad. As one special school head observes, 'It makes us wonder whether we ought to teach our children to read at all, if they are going to learn to enjoy books only to find as they reach their later teens there are no more books suitable for them'.

Books with easy vocabulary, not too much solid text and clear illustrations are nearly all for children. Characters, plot and pictures relate to the child's world, not the adult's. 'Coffee table' picture books serve for browsing, but not to satisfy the desire to *read*.

One area where children's books can prove suitable, in spite of 'CHILDREN'S' emblazoned on the covers, is the Bible. There is a wealth of Bible stories at all levels, from the toddlers' picture book through to the full text. The pictures show Bible characters – mostly adults.

Richard is a bookworm. He visits the public library most weeks, at present mostly choosing well-illustrated children's non-fiction, where again the pictures are not all of children. He and his younger friend, also with Down's Syndrome, get completely absorbed in cartoon books like *Asterix* and *Tin-Tin*. Virtually the only stories he actually reads are from his various children's Bibles. Those he loves. They are ideal for someone who has a fair reading vocabulary but cannot sustain the concentration for long. Most Bible stories are quite short. His favourite book, the *Ladybird Bible Story-book*, is reassuring because each story is complete within a single page spread. You never *have* to turn over. So Richard knows how much reading he is taking on when he begins. (Our copy has the ultimate accolade on the cover: 'God's own story *now on ITV*'. I always feel God must enjoy that!)

A literary sort of Englishwoman myself, I used to scorn the picture strip but now I am drawn to their shelves in continental bookshops – with Richard in mind. In Paris I bought a well-drawn picture-strip biography of Martin Luther King, thinking Keith would enjoy the French text. One day a year or two later the American martyr's name came up and we were surprised to find Richard knew the name and much of his story just from perusing those pictures. Oh for more, and with English captions he could read!

My husband left a couple of issues of *History Today* out for me one day. He was surprised to find one on his desk later with a request for a copy of page 37 in Richard's curious spelling. Richard had evidently been browsing and was fascinated by some pictures of unusual post boxes. A library book he once had on stamp collecting suggested that post boxes were also interesting to 'collect'. He has photographed a number himself and wished to add to these.

Friends in the church could consider whether they take any illustrated magazines which might be enjoyed later by those with limited reading skills. Sports, cars, gardening, fashion, pop – as appropriate to age and sex – might all be welcome. You may be surprised how pleased they are that anyone should think of them liking the printed page.

Helping them worship

Few Christians would question the need for pastoral concern for people with mental handicaps. Care is obviously appropriate. But people do question their ability to get much else from religion. Can it have any meaning for anyone with really restricted intellectual powers?

And then we go and sing about worshipping with heart and soul! It is not *only* a matter of mind and strength.

Love, the keynote of the gospel, can be conveyed to those

with the most minimal of responses. From there up, more and more becomes possible. Profoundly handicapped people can be capable of worshipping God. They can be swept up into the reverent atmosphere of praise and thanksgiving. They can be aware of something bigger beyond that which their senses register. 'The fact that we do not see anything does not mean that nothing is taking place. Even the silence of a disruptive child may be part of a profound religious experience'.[3]

We need to recognise that there are mentally handicapped people who, as one minister expressed it, 'are able to hear the resonance of the presence of God, when people thought they could not hear anything'.[4]

Supporting the families

This book is primarily concerned with the handicapped themselves, but the church can do, and sometimes sadly fails to do, much to support families with a handicapped member.

Families coming to terms with the fact that their child is handicapped will experience a range of feelings closely akin to bereavement, yet it is an ongoing experience in a different way. Parents often feel isolated. They are over-sensitive and easily hurt. Friends feel their own healthy children are almost an affront, and do not know what to say.

Joan Bicknell, a Professor of Psychiatry of Mental Handicap, explains:

> They will find great comfort if others will emphasise the 'ordinaryness' of the family and the child rather than the abnormality with which they are coming to terms. Families at this time describe how they are shunned by their neighbours and how, through embarrassment, those who used to speak pass hurriedly by. The warm welcome of such a child into the family of the Church . . . will do much to help the family find their own coping skills and keep in touch with the Church.[5]

Baptist ministers, questioned about the experience of parents in their churches, have observed:

They have been through the questions, such as 'Why has this happened? Why did God allow it?' The questions now are practical . . .

I think it helps the parents and the handicapped person to see that God loves them and their child individually and overwhelmingly.

The handicapped child has caused much heart-searching and even doubts about a simplistic fundamentalist faith, yet at the end of the day what emerges is a more assured, developed faith in the providence of an Almighty God.

For families to develop a more assured faith, they need supportive Christian friends. Perhaps more find these as public attitudes to the handicapped get more enlightened, but some parents have felt neglected, with no one to understand. It takes a strong faith to survive that.

Those left behind

Not everyone is able to move out into the community. Some will always be confined, even if in smaller units. Bryan George, author of *The Almond Tree: The Pastoral Care of Mentally Handicapped People*,[6] visited a hospital for mentally handicapped children and young people in the north of England. Afterwards he reflected:

I shall never forget the pride with which I was shown around, or the expression of happy contentment on the faces of the residents. As I approached this isolated complex of Victorian buildings, my heart sank. I need not have worried, for I discovered that a dedicated staff had transformed the interior with imagination, creating a pleasing and comfortable home out of some very institutional structures. This was *home* for over one hundred youngsters, providing shelter and food, loving care and security.

The chaplain was worried about his ministry now that less handicapped patients had moved out into the community. He had relied upon the more able residents to encourage and motivate the others but they were no longer there. I could sympathise, for as a teacher I had always found that in mixed-ability classes the less able pupil reached a higher level of attainment when stimulated by the brighter ones. This was easier for the teacher than trying to educate the bottom stream on their own.

As I continued my journey, I thought long and hard about what I had heard and seen. Like most people, I had welcomed the policy of moving those able to cope out of 'institutional care' and back into the community. Obviously I had certain reservations, which were confirmed by my visit to the hospital. I was told of the hostility encountered from anxious neighbours when trying to purchase suitable property. I could now understand the fears of those who had been moved; they would not have been very different from the residents I saw, who were happy, contented and secure. I was told about the careful way in which they were prepared for the move. Nevertheless, it must have been a very frightening experience. I resolved to do all I could to encourage Christians to be good neighbours, and make every effort to welcome these newcomers in to neighbourhood and church.

What I had not thought about before was the effect that this policy would have on those left behind. The difficulties that all staff, not just the chaplain, would encounter in serving the extremely handicapped alone. The patients had not just lost good friends, but fellow residents who were able to help and encourage them in a variety of ways.

Ought local churches to explore ways of ministering to 'the ones left behind' as well as those who are now endeavouring to settle into the community?

Some churches arrange visits to nearby hospitals. They too are going to find it more difficult and less rewarding as the more responsive move out. Yet they, children as well as adults, could be just what the chaplain needs to keep the songs moving and get these other children of God involved.

Supporting the carers

Some people find themselves challenged to go beyond easy kindness and consider working with the mentally handicapped. There is plenty of opportunity at a variety of levels: professional openings for teachers, nurses, social workers, but also work for carers and befrienders to help in homes, at day centres and clubs, paid or voluntary. You may not need a lot of special training, but you have to be a special kind of person to seek such work. Nobody finds it *easy*, but happily some find it satisfying and worthwhile.

Smaller units of care make extra demands on the staff, who work more intimately with fewer individual residents than in a big institution. The opportunities may be increased, but so is individual responsibility. It can be lonely as well as demanding work. This may lead to frequent staff changes, breaking the continuity of care. This is hard on the residents. It can also be difficult for outside bodies, like churches, who must repeatedly re-establish good relations.

Churches ought to recognise members involved with handicapped people – not just the parents, but all those who choose to work with them in any professional or voluntary capacity. In my own church in the last three or four years one member has been on the management committee setting up a Shaftesbury Home for mentally handicapped adults; another, formerly a laboratory technician, has joined the staff of a day centre, while her daughter is contemplating special needs teaching; an older lady was sad to retire from escort duties on a bus serving special schools; and a lecturer in home economics finds her duties include classes of students with severe learning difficulties. I doubt whether many of their fellow church members are aware of all this, but such people are expressing the love of Christ.

The church should care about its carers.

3

New Faces at Church

'I like church. I do like church', Richard has been heard to sing in the bath.

For him our church has always been a happy and liberating place. Liberating because from his early years he could escape from his parents there! We could let go of him because we could trust the church community as a whole to keep a protective eye on him. Within the church a surprising range of people have found time to help him, draw him out, teach him new skills. For us this has been a very real expression of Christian love, backing up both the strength we have found in our faith and the teaching Richard has received about Jesus.

Now Richard is pleased and proud to be a full member of the church, following believer's baptism, and he is eager to find ways in which he can serve. 'I try to be a useful church member,' he explains, 'because I love Jesus.' That is as far as he can go in articulating what it means to him. Much that is important to us passes over his head. So he throws himself into practical tasks which he can do perfectly well. We sense that these – clearing coffee cups, assisting the frail, handing out hymn books – are all part of his worship, his offering to Jesus. Going to church is an important part of his life.

A church which has no experience of handicapped worshippers but feels it ought to welcome people from the new hostel down the road may anticipate problems that will never arise. A church which has experience, good or bad, may assume other handicapped people will be like the first. That could be misleading.

No book can tell you what your new friends will be like. There is no substitute for getting to know them personally, so that you become aware of their various needs, problems, abilities, and gifts. It is possible, however, to suggest a few things for which you might be alert.

Welcoming the baby

Many parents, like us, have found their churches have welcomed and made room for their handicapped child. Perhaps at first people have been curious or embarrassed, but that has soon passed. As one mother put it,

> After the initial adjustment which folk had to make (to be able to 'look' and not be afraid, and realise she was not just some monster), everyone accepted her extremely well.

Listening to parents, it is disturbing to realise how often the best experiences of handicapped children lovingly received are related by families already deeply involved in the life of that church. The degree of handicap seems to be less relevant. Such parents expect their church to accept their child. That helps the church to respond positively.

Other parents tell sadder tales of churches that seem to have rejected their family. When they have enquired about infant baptism or dedication, they have been asked, 'What's the point – for a child like that?' If these parents are on the fringe of a church, perhaps attending quite often but not really drawn into the fellowship, they may drift away from the church altogether just when they could most do with friends.

It may be proper for the vicar to question why parishioners who do not otherwise appear at church want to have their babies baptised, but it cannot be right to turn a handicapped baby away because he may not grow up to understand. If we really doubt whether God has room in his church for such children, we shall indeed find it hard to have one fidgeting near us in the pew.

We should not get complacent because we hear more of the happier experiences. Few of the other families are still around the churches to tell their tale.

Bringing the child to church

Even if the church is welcoming, it may not be easy for the parents to bring a handicapped child to church. There may be physical problems of mobility or problems with disturbed and unsociable conduct. Some will be no more difficult than other children, though they take longer to outgrow childish behaviour. Frequent illness and other problems often associated with handicap may make regular attendance impossible: that makes it harder to get the child used to the pattern of Sunday. The more severe the handicap, the harder it is to adjust to anything new, so regular routines are a help and variations can be daunting.

Many are capable of controlled behaviour and take a pride in 'doing it right'. Some whose behaviour is disturbing may never have grasped what is expected of them. Others have real problems in controlling body and voice. How far other worshippers can bear with this seems to vary greatly from place to place.

David Wilson, a Roman Catholic priest experienced in this field, senses how parents feel:

> Parents are often worried if their child will not sit still, or remain silent, or attend to what is happening. It is impossible to be dogmatic here. There are degrees of disturbance. Perhaps it is more important for the parents to make sure that *their* attitude is correct, than to be always checking and scolding their youngster beside them. If Mum and Dad give themselves wholeheartedly to the Mass, their child may feel in his own way at certain moments that something important is taking place. This will be difficult for the parents at times, as they may be conscious of what others are thinking, as their youngster makes strange noises, or fidgets continually.
>
> But we don't go to Mass for a few moments of quiet prayer. Mass is for being together in our worship.[1]

Where parents stay with the church, the handicapped child can often fit into the regular provision for children. This may mean recruiting an extra helper. A crèche can usually cope with the baby, but it is hard if the crèche is expected to keep older children whose behaviour is unacceptable for a Sunday school class! Often the handicapped child will get along quite well in the younger Sunday school classes and enjoy the activities, especially if he has a special friend beside him to help him join in.

Parents cannot help feeling at times that they are imposing on their friends by expecting others to cope with the handicapped child. Parents know the difficulties only too well, so their anxious eyes and ears quickly pick up signs of exasperation. That makes friends who persist all the more precious.

Philip's mother tells how her Down's son was accepted in the primary class. 'I think they must have had the patience of Job to cope with him even for an hour.' A Sunday school teacher admits that he often drove them to distraction and periodically someone would exclaim, 'He'll have to go!' They persevered, and so did the Boys' Brigade in due course. Philip has grown up to be a loved member of that church.

At another church a newly-arrived family asked if the Sunday school would receive their difficult, severely handicapped daughter along with her brothers. The teachers were ready to try, found another helper, and did their best. Word soon went round that they could cope. In a short time the Sunday school had half a dozen handicapped children, which was very demanding but full of pastoral opportunities as they got to know families who had not expected anyone voluntarily to take on their children. The Sunday school leader and her teachers had no special training for such work. When they sought advice, they found that by instinct and common sense they were already doing most of the things a specialist teacher could suggest. A key factor was providing a helper specially responsible for each of these children, who could help them join in or withdraw them to a different activity as seemed appropriate.

Within the church context, special helpers do not need particular training and qualifications as long as they are kind, patient and willing. They can learn from parents about a child's special needs, how that child communicates, and what he or she can do. The child's school may also give useful advice. Sometimes the helper may need to learn a simple sign language. Should the child be prone to fits, the helper should be taught to cope with that. Occasionally the mother is very protective and reluctant to entrust her child to another's care. If she sees a friend really cares enough about the child, she may come to be very glad to be released for a little while.

Other children's reactions

Having a handicapped child in the class – or in the Brownie pack, Boys' Brigade, or whatever – asks a lot of the other children. Some people think it is best to say nothing and assume they will not notice. They will! It is much better to try to explain that Johnnie or Jennie has something wrong and cannot help the odd movements, funny speech or other peculiarities. Very young children can grasp the difference between someone deliberately acting silly to annoy and someone *unable* to do things properly.

A little child taught me that. From the start we tried to explain Richard's condition to his brother, who was three years older and quickly aware that something was amiss with his baby. Even so, I had not realised the wider need.

One day, when Richard was about three, I was pleased to see him playing with a neighbour's child of similar age. There was a knock at the door. Trudi stood there, and demanded straight out, 'Is there something wrong in Richard's head that he can't talk?' Startled by the blunt attack, I said 'Yes'. 'That's all right, then,' said Trudi. 'Now I know he's trying, not just being silly', and she went back to play. They remained friends until she moved away. Over the years other local children sought similar reassurance, but then made Richard welcome in their games.

Children are observant. It is not fair to expect them not to notice odd behaviour or slow development. I used to despair of the friends who would whisper kindly to me, 'We haven't said anything to the children about Richard.' It was often the signal for a difficult afternoon. It does help if they are taken into adult confidence and their sympathy is enlisted. Soon they will be taking a pride in the achievements of their handicapped friend.

Growing up

A little child, although handicapped, may fit into the younger Sunday school classes quite well, but as the years pass by the slower development becomes more apparent. It is tempting to let him stay back with rather younger children, especially if he can now understand the simple stories. That may be all right up to a point – but soon this young-for-his-years boy will reach puberty. Then you realise how inappropriate it is for a youth with deep voice, hairy chin and teenage interests to be in among younger children.

Generally the handicapped child is better among those nearest in age for all those activities in which he or she can share. Where they cannot keep up, ideally another helper will arrange something more suitable. Some, for instance, enjoy doing some Bible study like the others, but it needs to be at their level. There may need to be a judicious mixture of integration and separate activity.

In our church Richard happens to be an odd one out for age. For a long time he tagged on socially to his brother's friends, who would take him around, play snooker with him, and so on. When they departed to college, the next group was some years younger. They were friendly towards Richard, but he was a teenager while they were still children. As they grow older, they do more that he can join in. He seems to move freely between some of their activities (including a happy weekend youth hostelling) and a group in their twenties, counting both as his friends. When it comes to humping furniture about, there is no doubt that he is one of the strong young men of the church.

Louise is nineteen and accepted as part of the church family and young people's group. Her minister writes of her admiration for the parents:

Louise is given every encouragement to go away with friends and is given every confidence. What this risk-taking costs in anxiety and dedication I cannot say, but her parents remain positive and cheerful. In addition they have trained Louise painstakingly to read and to do the other habitual things which make her readily acceptable in a group. She is always ready to help, especially in the home, and works very well . . . We must support parents of mentally handicapped people and take some responsibility for caring sometimes so that they may have a break.

Louise came on our youth weekend in Devon this year, her second trip with our young people. She is very little trouble; in fact, the fully fit and totally competent youngsters are more trouble than Louise would ever be! The key to her inclusion in the group is to do with the attitude we try to foster on a much larger scale in the church: one of acceptance. The youth group chose the name 'The Mixed Bunch': they include Africans, Caribbean British, Irish and white British. Apart from Louise, they range from those whose educational opportunities were not very good through to an Oxford graduate. A friend in Devon said we are very lucky to have a church like this. I felt obliged to respond that although it is a blessing, it is not luck. We have to work very hard on acceptance and giving people a sense of personal worth.

Making adults welcome

Of course, it is easier when the handicapped child is brought along from babyhood and grows up used to the church. Those who come as adults, perhaps with others from a group home, may not be familiar with worship, or with the worship patterns of that church. If they have been used to a hospital service, geared to their needs, they may well want to continue going to church but find the change in style quite difficult.

Even so, we should not assume that it will be hard to incorporate them into the congregation. We may need to help them find their way through the service, and show them what is expected, yet not be too quick to discourage their own ways of expressing worship. We might even learn something from them.

One rather staid church was surprised when a young man from the local hostel brought the exuberant participation of his previous lively, charismatic fellowship into their worship. They soon got used to it, and he was not too put off by their more inhibited approach. When his mother visited, she wondered at the happy way they got on together.

Some handicapped adults – just like other people – choose not to go to church. A chaplain talking to some at a Training Centre was told by one man that he 'only liked to go on special occasions as he preferred to think things out for himself', while his friend explained, 'I don't know anyone there'.[2] Don't the excuses sound familiar?

Joining in, whatever the activity, is valued by many handicapped people (although some forms of mental handicap tend to isolate those afflicted). One church chuckles over the concert to which they invited residents of a neighbouring hostel. During proceedings the lady responsible for the concert party invited one of these friends to join her on stage. Whereupon a large number of the residents took their partners and the concert became almost a church dance!

Near another church a hostel for mentally handicapped adults opened about four years ago. The first warden was a church member. The minister reflects on this contact.

I remember his involvement in the selection of the first residents and how he visited large institutions at a distance with a view to bringing local people back home. Over the last year or so a number of residents have turned up in our congregation, sometimes escorted by staff, but lately coming on their own in ones or twos or in a larger group.

During the summer I felt I must do something to establish real friendship in addition to our meetings at church, so I invited them to the manse for lunch, together with a number of other people from the church. These latter admitted to a lack of confidence, but were very willing and by the end of the occasion everyone felt they had really grown in friendship. We are now trying to do more, making sure that our friends are included in our church events. In a forthcoming church outing we are able to include elderly people in wheelchairs and we hope to include friends from the hostel too as part of the family. We think we must avoid the temptation to organise special outings for these people, separated from the main family.

When a group come from the hostel, they need a lot of help from the congregation in finding hymns etc. and one of our people said, 'Can't we persuade them to spread about a bit so more people have a chance to help?' On reflection we concluded that, as they feel more confident, so the group will break up naturally and won't feel the need to sit together.

Participating in worship

Many mentally handicapped people can share in the worship of God. How much they understand is a different matter – and may not be particularly relevant. Worship is not just of the mind. It also involves heart and soul. Feelings, instinct, intuition can all be active where the intellect is weak, and these are all involved in worshipping God.

Most people with a mental handicap are sensitive to atmosphere, including the atmosphere of reverence. That alone is quite challenging to other worshippers!

A hospital chaplain observes that it is always possible to tell when there are Christians among the staff present in the chapel. Sometimes none of the attendant staff have any interest in worshipping God. They may even talk through the prayers, which is no help to others. In the local church it ought to be easier to achieve a congregational atmosphere conducive to worship.

Yet in that hospital chapel David always raises his arms in praise. No one else around does. It seems to be an instinctive response to God.

The chapel has a fine stained glass window depicting Jesus and the children. Although high up, it commands attention. The chaplain has observed several handicapped worshippers gazing at this window, entranced. As Sarah looked at it, her usual bewildered expression changed for a few moments to 'the look of one seeing Christ'.

It is easy to assume that much in our services will be unintelligible to them *and therefore boring*. We may not be allowing for their sense of the presence of God. We may underestimate their sense of belonging and so being part of what is going on. We probably judge their boredom threshold by our own. It is quite possible that the boredom of words washing over them, words which they do not understand, is so much part of their lives anyway, that it is less irritating to them than those with more active minds imagine.

Richard, who has a considerable ability to sleep anywhere any time if bored, copes simply with long Baptist sermons. At the first note of the organ he is awake again, beaming happily, for the next hymn. I suppose it is not really so different from me, hopelessly unmusical, 'switching off' during a choral anthem. Probably we all find some parts of a service speak more directly to us than do others.

Mentally handicapped worshippers grasp best the concepts of praise, thanksgiving and intercession. Many love the familiar Lord's Prayer, usually referred to as 'Our Father', though Richard hooked on to it as the 'Thy Kingdom Come' prayer. They may learn the words of this, and of other frequently used prayers and simple hymns, and love to use them. Churches using a regularly repeated liturgy have the advantage here.

A hospital chaplain observes that her congregation learns to recognise new hymns and prayers quickly. There is hardly anything they can understand, but she does not feel that matters. She chooses hymns with tunes they will enjoy, often with actions, and hopes the words speak to the staff. The hymns are rendered like 'bel canto' singing – all tune and vowels, without consonants or meaning. Some dance, some run up to the altar rails. They feel the sense of worship.

It will not always be easy to move from that to worship in a local church. Churches, however, can get used to quite a lot if they want to. Jack has moved happily from hospital chapel to local church. He is wary of new tunes but lets rip on those he knows in a loud falsetto, slightly off-key. At first people noticed, uncomfortably, but now the church would hardly feel right without it!

The style of worship in some churches may appear better suited to mentally handicapped people than that in others. Repeated liturgies with plenty of symbolic action can be helpful. So can lively charismatic worship. Probably nothing sounds less promising than a traditional Baptist service, rather static and full of words, but there are plenty, like Richard, happy to be part of such worship. Probably we all look at our handicapped friends struggling with our pattern and imagine that the grass might be greener for them somewhere else.

The style of worship is really less important than the sense of belonging. The attitude of people around is crucial. If other people are easily disturbed, it makes it harder for those sitting with someone who cannot keep quiet and still. The handicapped themselves will probably sense the irritation and feel unwanted.

Isn't it hard not to look round when you hear a bit of a disturbance in church? Do you turn with a friendly smile or a frown?

Frances Young, a Methodist minister with a severely handicapped son, observes that it is all right taking Arthur to churches where they are known, but she would hesitate to take him on a first visit to an unfamiliar Methodist church. Visiting a black church, she would happily take him along:

> One of the liberating features of the independent black churches is the noise and exuberance of their worship, their acceptance of every one of us, with joy and love and concern, Arthur included. There is no sense there of forcing Arthur on people who would rather not know and cannot cope.[3]

Attitude is paramount. That is a challenge to us all.

One Sunday two residents from the neighbouring hostel came into evening worship. The minister remembers it thus:

> Late, noisy, *very* smartly dressed, they sat right in front – utterly at home. One is almost inarticulate yet loves to communicate – and sing! We had to concentrate to worship and hoped he would gradually settle down. He did. Not a sound in prayers or reading. They are very responsive to 'atmosphere'. There was some chipping in during the sermon but that may be no bad thing – perhaps more people should do it!

Disturbance

People get worried about the possibility of disturbances. In fact the mentally handicapped are not the only people who can disturb a service. A good many of them will never do so, but some will and this has to be faced.

40

For a start, the attentive ones will probably take every-thing at its face value. Ministers chuckle about the shock of having all their rhetorical questions answered. They soon learn to beware of including too many in the sermon! When one asked the children, 'Did you wash your hands before you came out?' Maud, who lives in the group home across the road, decided hers were dirty. She made a noisy exit on her walking frame and a similar re-entry, clean, ten minutes later.

An answer to a question that expected no reply may amuse the congregation – and spoil a serious point. Irrelevant shouts can cause a worse disturbance. David loves the service at the hospital chapel. He 'shadows' vocally, echoing the words. Yet he can still cry out in the middle, 'Judy, what we doing tomorrow?' And, the chaplain ruefully admits, it is a distrac-tion. How much more a distraction in a local church, beyond the hospital walls.

It is hard to get churches to admit to serious problems. They would much rather recount stories of successful in-tegration, but doubtless there are plenty of private grouses. One Baptist Superintendent (a senior minister with responsi-bilities to help churches over a wide area) describes a problem he has met.

Fulfilling a preaching engagement in one of our Baptist churches, I was made aware of the problems that can be associated with the church and mental handicap. The church was a fairly large one and it had a genuine concern for the community in which it was placed. Part of that concern was expressed in links which had been established with a local hospital for the mentally handicap-ped. As a result of that ministry, a man and a woman, both in their late twenties and both quite severely mentally handicapped, had become regular members of the morning congregation. They sat together in the front pews and obviously thoroughly enjoyed the service. During the hymns, they certainly 'made a joyful noise unto the Lord', but it was so unmusical that it disturbed those who had even a slight sense of harmony. The greatest distraction, however, was experienced during the sermon. They were unable to concentrate upon what was being said and spent the entire time in very loud conversation with each other, accompanied by frequent gestures of the arms and intermittent giggling. This behaviour made it impossible for many of the other members of the congregation to follow what was being said and even the preacher found it difficult to maintain the train of thought. The situation had reached the point where some, even of the most loyal members of the church, were indicating that they would have to consider worshipping elsewhere.

In these circumstances, the church officers faced a very real dilemma. They sympathised with those who felt that the distraction made it difficult, perhaps impossible, to give full attention to the worship. At the same time the officers were anxious not to turn away two people for whom worship and contact with other people obviously meant so much.

Several ways had been suggested for dealing with the situation. A trusted member of the congregation had tried sitting with the couple in an attempt to minimise the disturbance but this had only resulted in increased disruption as they loudly demanded explanations. The church officers were unwilling to arrange for them to go out when the Junior Church left the sanctuary for classes, as part of their enjoyment was in being treated as adults. A hint that they might sit at the back had been stoutly resisted.

It was a dilemma for which the church and its officers had found no satisfactory answer.

It is hard to see a satisfactory solution when a situation has been allowed to develop like that. Whether their behaviour could have been modified acceptably at an earlier stage, one cannot tell. Sometimes, if you know the people, you can envisage some of the potential problems and may be able to avoid them. But many mentally handicapped people just are unpredictable.

One church with a number of handicapped worshippers finds that most present few problems, but Sandra is difficult. In her early twenties, she comes from a violent home, with her father often in prison. Sandra has attended the special Bible class since she was sixteen and comes to the Sunday services, morning and evening, often arriving half an hour early. When she feels unwell or unsettled she does various things to gain attention, especially during the sermon. Often she bangs the heating pipes, which make a resounding noise all along the row, or she may bang the umbrella stands. One week she bit her hymn book as noisily and obviously as she could.

> This produces a real dilemma. We say we expect 'acceptable' behaviour from our handicapped friends as part of our treating them as normally as possible. This isn't acceptable as it puts the minister off, and various members of the congregation. But Sandra is there and, although not having committed herself, is drawn to faith. We try to give her lots of attention in other ways to try to lessen the need for this attention-seeking. We are not sure how to react. If we get cross, this is what she wants. Does it matter if she eats hymn books? We feel it does when it disturbs the worship. Problem unsolved!

Communication – verbal and physical

Often the difficulty may lie not in a basic refusal to co-operate but rather in a failure to understand what is required. Even relatively 'bright' handicapped people, with quite good language development, need guidance expressed in *very clear, simple, firm instructions*. As a parent, you realise painfully how strict you have to make yourself sound to get the message across. It is just no good saying pleasantly, 'Would you mind doing . . .' because the point is lost in among all those words, and gentle hints are useless. Kindly people often fail to realise this. If we want to broach a delicate matter, we often wrap it up in courteous phrases. Before deciding that handicapped friends cannot or will not behave more acceptably, it is important to check whether they have understood or whether they might if it was tackled in a different way. The staff who care for them might be able to help here.

Body language needs to match our words. Expressions, gestures and tone of voice all convey the message more clearly than the phrases used, so it is important that they convey it right. It is no good expressing a welcome without a smile, as you shrink away from a warm embrace. A disciplining 'No!' needs to sound determined enough to be understood.

A measure of control can be exercised, though that will be harder if undesirable habits get established. In any case, it must be recognised that there is a limit to the amount of restraint that can be imposed on those who do not understand.

Someone stern trying to insist on something just might provoke an aggressive outburst, which could be nasty. Again it comes back to knowing the individuals. They will respond better to those whom they have learned to like and trust. Friends may have to think carefully about what is tolerable and what really is unacceptable, and concentrate on improving a little at a time.

Kevin lives in a community home and goes to a church which, like Sandra's, has a Bible class for mentally handicapped adults. He clearly feels at home in the church, as the class leader describes:

He will pop into the church building if he sees it open during the day. He has now accepted that not every meeting at the church is open for everyone to attend: 'Mothers and Toddlers' and the Deacons' Meeting are restricted to certain groups of people!

Kevin has a problem with time-keeping, usually arriving far too early, often before the door is open. Arriving an hour early for the 11 o'clock service can create problems when there is a 9.30 service still in progress. I felt that it was a little disconcerting when Kevin arrived during the sermon, entering by the side door which leads straight into the church. To reach his usual seat he had to walk across the church between the communion table and the front pew. He would not proceed until his presence had been acknowledged by the organist and preacher. Our own minister knew what to expect, but visiting preachers were taken by surprise.

I decided to discuss this with Kevin, stressing the times of the services and suggesting that if he arrived during the early service he could sit in the hall until coffee was served. Then I pointed out to him that we had a back door to the church which was often used by latecomers. I went outside with him and showed him the notice which was put up by the door when a service had begun. I went in the door, up the stairs at the back of the church and showed him how to reach his usual seat. He listened, followed me and nodded in understanding.

But the next Sunday in came Kevin during the 9.30 service, through the side door, across the front of the church and to his usual seat. I suppose that I felt slightly disappointed that he had not remembered what I had explained so carefully the previous Sunday. I decided that having shown him the alternative I would have to leave the decision to him in future.

There may be problems, but plenty of churches have not had major difficulties. The fear of disturbance easily gets out of proportion. Perhaps it is salutary to note that it is not all one-sided. One handicapped lady, who liked the idea of going to church, hesitated because 'I am afraid of having a turn and people would not understand.'[4]

Hugs and kisses

'No one told me they'd hug me!' remembers one hospital chaplain. It came as a physical shock and took a lot of getting used to. He has always been careful to prepare others for it since.

People whose means of self-expression are restricted are likely to show their emotions in physical ways. Anger may be released in physical aggression. More often it is the physical demonstration of friendship that other people find difficult to accept. It can be startling, to say the least, to meet adults who want to greet all and sundry with hugs and kisses. Richard has gradually been persuaded that grown-up Englishmen shake hands rather than kiss one another and that you need to know ladies pretty well before you greet them with a hug, but we see how important physical contact is to him even though he can talk to people quite well. I try to encourage him to keep his arms to himself – and then feel chastened when old ladies call me over to say how lovely it is when he throws his arms round them and kisses them, and I realise that they enjoy the rare warmth of a physical embrace.

Quiet guidance

A church may need to work out how best to help, and if necessary control, handicapped worshippers. The pastor of a small Merseyside church, which has successfully integrated a number into its life, suggests a helpful approach.

In services they sit together, and any help that they may occasionally require is given by other members, who sit close by, but not next to, our Mencap friends. We seek to treat them as the adults that they are.

In a supportive atmosphere some will be enabled to do more. We hear of a number of people with Down's Syndrome who are delighted to take up the congregation's offering. Usually this is something they can manage well, as in the church just mentioned. The pastor describes how:

> On the first occasion that Doreen took the offering, she did it with such dignity and bowed with great reverence to the Communion Table. I was so overcome with both joy and empathy that I could hardly frame the words for the prayer of thanks.

At another church Simon does the job with equal solemnity, but cannot resist a thumbs-up of innocent satisfaction to the congregation as he returns down the aisle.

This is lovely as long as people do not encourage them to think it funny. Sometimes clowning can become a problem. Many people with Down's Syndrome are great mimics and enjoy making people laugh. Friends tend to play up to this and have a good laugh all round, but it must not be allowed to go over the top. Otherwise what starts innocently enough can develop into a problem. One chaplain sees uneasily that some helpers' bows are more to the audience than the altar, 'milking' appreciation.

This chaplain adds a word of caution about live microphones. Down's mimics may seize upon a microphone and go into a pop star act. If this is likely, it is as well to switch them off quickly at the end of the service. On one occasion a young Down's clown began to chant a newly acquired phrase into a mike in the hospital chapel. To the chaplain's horror, the departing congregation was exhorted to leave with a repeated, obscene injunction. Since then it has been Benediction, Amen, and unplug.

Understanding

How much can the handicapped understand? That is another favourite question. It is not easy to answer, but it is clear that many grasp something of what worship is about.

We can try to use simple, straightforward language, we can ensure that there is something in the service in which they can join, but we should not get paranoid about making them understand. Understanding is not our responsibility. We can leave that to God. A sense of participation has something to do with the gospel.

Most handicapped people will like to be given a hymn book, the same as everyone else, even if they cannot read and hold it upside down. Some are aware that it is 'infra-dig' not to read, so it is important to look as if they are. Increasingly these days, the more able can read. Richard will quickly scan a hymn for word length and decide whether it is worth trying to sing along. If not, he will probably follow the words while we sing. If I know the words so do not bother to turn over promptly, he will swiftly do it for me.

Some can find the numbers, even if reading is difficult, and to do that much is important to them. So Ruth, wanting to help a fellow member who is blind, found the pages for her in hymn book and Bible, 'because she couldn't see the numbers'!

Limited understanding can, of course, give problems even with those who mean well and try to fit in, as another class leader explains:

Norman is in his mid-thirties and has Down's Syndrome. In his own words, he is high grade. He can read and write pretty well, reads William Barclay commentaries, and has been a long-standing, devoted member of the Bible class for eighteen years, and a church member for three. His mother is a forceful character who has brought Norman up to believe in himself and to achieve the most he can. This, alas, shows itself in an attitude of great self-righteousness. *He* has been to church and class all these years and must therefore be a very good person. Admittedly, he doesn't 'murder, steal' etc. but his pride is awful! Once when I was teaching and trying to get the point home, I said, 'I do lots of wrong things – don't you, Mrs Smith?' (appealing to another leader). 'Well,' says Norman, 'we are not all like you, you know!' (The point had *not* got across – as usual.)

When interviewing Norman for baptism and church membership there was no doubt of his faith in God and trust in Jesus as Lord and Saviour. We had to accept his other attitudes as part of his handicap and seek to modify them as best we could – but he does put people off coming. He is at present very upset that no one has asked him to be a deacon! [*One of the committee elected by a Baptist church to manage its day-to-day affairs.*] It is not the fact that he is handicapped that prevents this, it is his attitudes and we've had to tell him so, kindly but firmly.

There may be hiccups, yet many people with quite severe handicaps fit quietly into church life and appreciate belonging, without presenting real problems. Often it is those who are generally more able but still of limited understanding who prove the most testing of Christian patience. Many churches will know someone like Lynne.

Lynne is in her mid-forties, a victim of encephalitis in days before pressure-relieving shunts were invented. Bright and intelligent in many childish ways, her inadequacy lies in her emotional development, which is like that of an eight-year-old. She is deaf and has a loud, loud voice. She also has a fixation on Israel, the Bible land. Her minister describes how

She toddles in to *everything* (unless of course she is ill when she rings up to tell us – at least once and often twice, and that is an experience!). She arrives in her woolly hat (winter and summer) with an enormous bag with Bible, hymn book, and you name it. She plonks herself in the front row and makes sure there is a spare chair beside her on which to place her goods and chattels. She then goes out again to the kitchen to get a glass of water, which also goes on the chair beside her. If she doesn't hear the number of the hymn (which is frequently) she asks, loudly. During the address, which she cannot hear, she often either turns up her hearing aid until it shrieks, or else she falls asleep and snores loudly. At the end of whatever meeting it is she swans up to the minister and says, gripping him in vice-like talons, 'Now you know what you need now, Mr Clark, you need a good rest.' This is her basic maternalism. At the other end of the scale is her coquette act and she responds girlishly to teasing, 'Oooh, I could shoot you!'

And why tell this rather commonplace tale? First, to show how the church has learned to love. The Sisterhood grumbles like mad but makes sure that Lynne is never left out. The young people take her around with them. And so on. The second reason explains the first. She is God's gift to us, for let there be a prayer circle, quietly murmuring their requests to the Lord, which Lynne could not possibly hear physically, and at the right time Lynne will pick up her hymn book or her Bible and read exactly the right thing, God's word for that moment.

Then there are people like Alex, a man in his forties who has Down's Syndrome. He belongs to the same church as Norman and Sandra.

He was baptised and became a church member a few years ago. His worshipful attitude, especially at the communion service, is an inspiration to many. He makes up his own hymns which he sings a great deal.

For some years, while his father was terminally ill, he prayed devotedly for him each morning, but was content when his father did not recover.

Alex is a very humbling Christian man, a great pleasure to know.

4
What Can the Church Do for Them?

When Keith went away to university, Richard missed him sorely. The brothers had always been close so Richard was swept up into many of Keith's activities. Now he was left behind. His school and therefore his schoolfriends were at a distance, his beloved cousins live far away, and although neighbouring children were friendly he no longer had a special companion here. It was hard to be stuck with his parents, the 'older generation'.

'Coming for a walk, Richard?' 'Shall we have a game of snooker this afternoon?' One of the young men at church, recently married, was really kind to Richard in those first weeks when Keith and his friends had departed to college. Gary stepped into the breach on Sundays and helped Richard find a new niche among the young adults.

Richard clearly feels that he belongs to that group within the church now and they are lovely in their welcome to him, unperturbed when he flings his arms round them or dozes on their shoulders. The happy relationship has developed naturally, given the initiative of two or three perceptive friends who felt for him. Not all their activities are appropriate, but they are quick to include him in those that are. They tell him their news and take an interest in his. They welcome his help with various jobs, treating him as a responsible adult yet ready to be responsible for him when necessary. They are real friends.

Accept them

Exuberance apart, Richard is competent socially. Even so, such integration has been a pleasant surprise to us. With more severe handicaps it gets harder, but it is surprising what can be done if the will is there.

Ideally people with handicaps, physical as well as mental, will be accepted with a minimum of fuss about the disability and a maximum appreciation of them as individuals. If adult, they must be accepted as adults, whatever their 'mental age'. The limitations imposed by the condition have to be recognised but need not be dominant in all dealings with them.

When my father lost his sight, we had to learn not to say 'Look at this', 'See that', but rather to describe what we saw. If my sister and I were admiring our mother's new dress, he could sit in the corner and feel left out or we could tell him what it was like and he could imagine how it suited her.

Similarly Jane, asking her Sunday school class some questions about the story, knows that little Sally cannot take much of it in. She could pass her by quietly, or she could say to the others 'Sally won't understand', or she might think of a question that Sally probably could respond to. 'How many sheep did the shepherd shut up in the pen, John?' 'Ninety-nine.' 'Yes. Was the shepherd happy, Megan?' 'No, 'cos one was lost.' 'What did the lost sheep *say*, Sally?' 'Baa.' 'Good', and Sally baas to herself with satisfaction as the lesson continues.

Some congregations will be acutely aware of anyone 'odd' in their midst, their enjoyment of the hymns marred by one discordant singer, their concentration broken by grunts and restless movement from one corner. Other congregations seem able to take such things in their stride. One minister visiting a small church recently found that, of a congregation of thirty, nine were mentally handicapped – and no one thought it peculiar or special. Coming from outside, he noticed it, and also noted that they really were an integral part of that church.

Some churches nominate particular friends, ideally more than one, to relate to each handicapped person in their midst. That can be very helpful. Elsewhere it might be restricting, because the whole church takes these people to its heart.

We observe that Richard finds it important to know people

51

by name. He reproves me for not knowing the names of all the people who serve us in the local shops, railway stations and so on. He has a point, but I still do not find myself able to confront them all in his direct manner: 'Hullo, I'm Richard Bowers. What's your name?'

Putting a name to someone helps us to see him or her as a person, not just a representative ticket inspector, postman, cripple or idiot. Within the family of the church it ought to be possible to accord people this mark of individuality. Yet what do we hear?

> A mother, a fairly regular churchgoer, after the birth of her son, was known to the congregation not by her name but as 'the mother of that funny boy.'[1]

It's so easy to slip into this trap, isn't it? Knowing someone by name is a significant step in recognition and acceptance.

Not underestimate them

Martin is very severely handicapped in mind and body. His parents care for him devotedly. When well enough he attends the day centre and the Roman Catholic church. One day the new priest called. He chatted to Martin's mother and smiled at the boy lying there so helpless. As he left he said, kindly, 'Ah well, Mrs Price, at least you have the consolation of knowing that Martin is wholly without sin.' Suddenly Martin was in a frenzy, all noise and movement. His mother could not calm him. Gradually she came to believe he must somehow have sensed something of that remark or of her tense reaction. Was his very anger a claim to the human capacity for sin? In the end the parents took him to a monastic house they knew, where an hour or two of holy peace calmed his spirit.

If I just read that account, I should find it hard to believe. I heard it from the mother and could see that she too found it almost incredible, yet true.

The consolation that mentally handicapped people are 'holy innocents', incapable of sin, is offered to parents frequently and very kindly. Many parents find it disquieting. We may not want our children to sin but there is something dehumanising about not being capable of it.

Mothers of handicapped children often enjoy sharing tales of deliberately naughty behaviour. It is reassuringly normal. We could always tell whether or not Richard knew he was transgressing the 'rules'. If punished for something he did not realise was wrong, he used to cry. If he was deliberately provoking us, probably as a bid for attention, he would receive punishment without a flicker. It was maddening, but revealing.

Handicapped adults often have a moral feeling for good and bad. This moral sense may only operate within restricted bounds, and some are not capable of it at all, but those who can feel guilty and can feel sorry do not want or need that to be denied.

Character is not just a matter of intellect, and if handicapped people appear to have pleasing personalities it is a bit hard to write that off as part of their 'mindless' condition.

Help the family

A mother, on hearing that a priest was willing to visit her at home, replied:

> Wearied as I am with the burden of constant care, I would not welcome your visit if you came to dispense platitudes. But if you could offer to take care of my son for a few hours, that would be a different matter.[2]

A great burden of care falls upon the families of the handicapped. Today's policies encourage parents to keep their child at home. Few beyond the families realise what this means. Severe mental handicaps often go hand in hand with physical ones. Heart conditions, blindness, deafness, lack of control over limbs, double incontinence, epilepsy, these and other problems occur, sometimes several together. All this on top of having a child who may be unresponsive, with whom communication is difficult, and who probably has poor sleep patterns: it is daunting and exhausting.

A healthy child with a fair level of understanding, like Richard, is not so difficult, only making the demands of a rather younger child. Even so, we lost plenty of sleep at times. We would wake to records playing full blast at 2 a.m., the house vibrating to his joyful dance, or once to anguished sounds from the lavatory, choking over his attempts to flush away evidence of his early breakfast – several banana skins! In a spacious 'semi' he probably did not disturb the neighbours' sleep too, but imagine life in the middle of a block of flats . . . One father was regularly driven to walk the streets at midnight, pushing his son's wheelchair to keep the boy quiet.

Tim, another child with Down's Syndrome, favoured nocturnal bicycle rides round the local streets. His family developed a nightly security programme worthy of Fort Knox.

The more severe the handicap or behaviour problems, the harder it is to ask friends to babysit, especially when the 'baby' becomes a hefty adolescent. Anyone who cares enough to learn to cope (as parents have to) and offers to help out, even for an hour or two, is a great blessing.

Brothers and sisters share in the burden of caring. 'I remember thinking how left out she was, but also how demanding it was to look after her, even for a short while,' reflects an elder sister. It is particularly hard when a younger sibling has to be responsible for the older, their proper roles reversed.

When Keith was twelve, a schoolmaster asked us whether he was the oldest of a large family. No, we said, there was only one younger, but he had Down's Syndrome. 'That figures,' said the teacher, 'I knew something had made that boy too mature for his years.' That too is sad for the parents.

Sadder still to hear of a loving family with two handicapped children where the stresses have led to the normal older sister, still a little child, needing psychiatric treatment.

Where the handicapped child, or adult, is cared for at home, the practical help may well be directed more to parents and others in the family. Anything that reduces the overall stress and weariness will in the long run be beneficial to the handicapped person too.

Not all parents, or brothers and sisters, find their faith stands up to the test. Some tell of such lack of support from their churches that it is little short of a miracle where faith has survived. The mother of a severely handicapped woman writes of

> help so desperately needed and never received from the church. We had a very strong faith which stood us in good stead. But what people don't understand is that the whole family is handicapped. And it's very important that people understand that, especially the church. But ministers shy away from the subject: they don't know what to say.

Not everyone will be able to give practical help, probably very few will, but all in a church should care. Prayer is a practical and powerful form of support, when it comes from hearts that feel for the situation. It is tragic when a father, deeply involved in the life of his church, can observe that in the thirty-four years of his autistic son's life 'only on one occasion have prayers been said for him in our church, and this from a church that prides itself, quite justly, on its caring and sharing ministry.' The son has lived in a hospital since the age of nine, so has not been visible to the church, but the father's involvement with Mencap activities locally must have been known to the church.

'My faith had remained strong,' he writes, 'but sadly my wife began to question hers very deeply and began to worry about the future. At this point the church family should have been of real help. It wasn't, and the minister didn't even offer a prayer.' His wife died prematurely, and 'once again it was not the church that helped me' but people at work. That is the grim testimony of a still devoted and active member of the church.

Help the group home

Where handicapped people are settled together in group

homes or hostels the scope for practical support is wide. Church friends will need to get in touch with the staff to discover what kind of help is most useful. These may be fairly able people 'on their own' who would be glad of help and advice in various neighbourly ways. Others, less able, will have staff to keep the home running smoothly, but will still be glad of friends. In some homes staff change fairly often and the continuity of local friends may be valued.

One church found the staff at the home nearby were a bit suspicious of their interest at first, but relations eased as the staff saw the church folk were genuinely friendly and the residents were really made welcome at a range of church activities. Before long staff were glad to see visitors from the church, not least as friends to whom they could grouse about the unkind attitudes residents had experienced in the community at large.

Where there are not residential staff, handicapped neighbours may appreciate help or advice with all manner of daily activities: cooking, gardening, decorating, using public transport, coping with correspondence. They will have been trained in all the essential areas, but that will not cover everything that arises in daily life. They may like to be shown how to cook a new dish, or told about plants that flourish in local conditions, or introduced to local activities.

In some areas there are befriending schemes, like 'Friends for Friends'. Elsewhere it depends on individual initiative. Everywhere there will be a role for those who are ready imaginatively to seek ways to help handicapped neighbours get more out of life.

Make church resources available

This may be done by welcoming them into existing activities or by making special provision. The former suits today's stress on integration and normalisation, but there are still times when special provision is appropriate.

As well as the services of worship, many churches have a range of activities, regular and occasional, from play groups to pensioners' lunch clubs, from Harvest Supper to young people's hike. Almost any of these might absorb one or more handicapped people of the appropriate age, sex or fitness.

Down's Syndrome may slow little Leroy's learning process, but does not prevent him from working for some Cubs' badges. Josie managed to learn her Brownie promise – but the need to learn verbal formulas can be a barrier for some who could otherwise enjoy participating in such organisations.

Richard's youth club is not attached to the church, but is for participants in the Duke of Edinburgh's Award Scheme. He joins in much of what the more able young people do and loves it. He accepts that some things are beyond him, and that the others will tease him if he gets over-excited and behaves oddly, but they are friendly and he tries to conform. He has been swimming and ice skating with them, to the theatre and even to a member's birthday disco. After the bronze award expedition (two days hiking with camping gear in backpacks which Richard, not a great walker, must have found tough) the other boys made a point of telling his father how well he had done. He had tired but stuck at it with determination. They were proud of him. Many churches run youth clubs which might similarly absorb one or two handicapped young people.

A city centre church which runs a coffee lounge during the week finds a local special school glad to bring senior pupils there to practise social skills. It is an advance on role play in the classroom and less 'threatening' than a commercial café.

Another church planned a Bank Holiday ramble. Realising that none of their handicapped friends were walkers, they had not said much about this. As they gathered outside the church, they were dismayed to see Harry approaching, wearing trainers and carrying a packed lunch. He must have managed to read the notices and had got himself there, suitably equipped, at the right hour. Their horror was due to his very slow pace. Harry is over fifty and not used to walking. The route planned was long and in places would be a steep scramble.

As Harry slowly advanced, the party divided. One group said they could not possibly leave him out, the other protested that it would be cruel to take him as he could not keep up. The minister eventually decreed that it was impractical to take him and sent his wife to explain to the hostel staff. Then a member, dropping off some of the family, said she was taking an older friend to join the others for lunch and offered to take Harry then. The hostel warden rescued Harry, and they explained the new arrangements, which worked happily. Next time they plan a church outing, they will be careful to build in provision for any hostel residents who would like to join in.

In the winter this church arranged a series of family Sunday afternoons. The adults watched a film series on family life, then had tea, all pooling their contributions, followed by a time of discussion. Meanwhile, in a second room, a children's film was shown, with an interval to join the adults for tea. Finally all came together for a short act of worship. The hostel residents naturally attended, but were quite content to watch the children's film as the more enjoyable for them. They were not the only adults in the second room, for several others watched this film while keeping an eye on the children. Jostling at the buffet did not appeal to the handicapped group, who preferred to keep their own packed teas and friends brought them drinks.

With goodwill all round and the recognition that just to participate is important, it is surprising what scope there is in church life.

Special provision

Some churches find there are a number of handicapped people in their area and decide to make some special provision. Again this can take a variety of forms. It is largely a matter of finding out what the needs are and responding imaginatively. A number of fellowships which have taken up the idea of a church audit find that, when they enquire about local community needs, provision for the mentally handicapped is suggested.

Some churches run clubs for handicapped children, young people or adults. These may be weekly or monthly, all round the year, or holiday clubs which take children for two or three days a week in school holidays. Churches often have suitable premises and equipment (like snooker, table tennis, records for dancing, etc. from the regular youth club). It requires a lot of helpers, sometimes achieved by ecumenical effort: one club uses Baptist premises, Methodist caterers, Roman Catholic transport, and friends from all the churches prepared to assist. Even the more able appreciate a high staffing ratio, as they love to talk to someone with time to listen.

A few churches hold special Bible classes for mentally handicapped adults and find this both possible and appreciated, although the ability range covered by 'severe learning difficulties' can seem pretty daunting. A leader describes a typical prayer time:

'Pray to God. I'm glad people are coming to my house to tea. Amen,' says sociable Susan.

'Auntie. Amen,' says John, and in that one word thanks God for the lady who looks after him and asks God to bless her.

Then Mary prays a longer prayer, complete with lines from choruses and verses of Scripture.

The longevity and popularity of some of the existing classes suggests that much more could be done in this field, perhaps ecumenically. There could be more for handicapped children too. The mother of two autistic little boys explains that they cannot be accepted in the local Sunday school as their behaviour is too anti-social. Yet at home 'we have prayers together every day with a Bible story and children's hymns . . . Would it be feasible for the churches to consider holding a Sunday school in a central town and picking up those mentally handicapped who would benefit by minibus or cars and taking them home again? If it was only once a month it would be useful. Also a simple service for mentally handicapped adults in this way would help these often lonely folk and give them hope for the future.' It can be done and is appreciated, but such efforts demand considerable long-term commitment.

Quite a lot of churches now arrange an occasional 'Mencap' service to which mentally handicapped people are invited. It is planned with simple and lively content to interest them. These are probably best where linked with an ongoing concern for the handicapped, and their value lies not just in what is offered to the handicapped but also in making others more aware of them.

Churches often realise that a one-off burst of activity is not much help but find the prospect of on-going heavy commitment daunting. Two examples show what can be done with a level of involvement many churches might manage. It is important to assess in advance the time commitment people can make, as well as their goodwill. It is possible to achieve continuity without too frequent demands on volunteers.

One house group included a man who worked at the local hostel for mentally handicapped adults. The group became interested and wondered what might be done to help. They decided to invite the dozen residents and six staff to a Sunday lunch at the church. A member of the group remembers how

> We approached this with some degree of apprehension. Face to face with these people, how would we cope? What could we say? Could we cope with a sudden outburst of 'strange' behaviour?
>
> We found it easier than we imagined to get alongside them. So the atmosphere was TENSE before they arrived, it gradually became RELAXED, and ended on a HAPPY note.

After a good lunch which they all enjoyed,

> Some of the more agile members of the house group and residents played basketball in the school hall. This was very enjoyable, if somewhat noisy!

The house group has since arranged other lunches, roughly once a quarter, and has got to know some of the hostel residents quite well. One or two occasionally attend the church and are accepted. The congregation has got used to the youth with a very loud laugh thirty seconds after everybody else's (sometimes handicapped people do not 'get' the joke at all, but like to join in the pleasant atmosphere of laughter). The group arranged a New Year party for them, with a disco following the meal. 'This was great fun.'

My correspondent offers this advice from their experience:

Don't be afraid.

These people have great capacity for affection.

Find out what they can do and what their interests are.

Pray for them.

Don't let whatever you do be a one-off effort – try to establish a continuity of concern.

At another church the Women's Meeting was challenged by a conference speaker to consider inviting mentally handicapped people to tea, but the women felt 'numerically and physically inadequate' for such an effort. Instead they shared the concern with the rest of the church and then approached the local Social Services with a tentative offer to do *something*. The voluntary services co-ordinator suggested that parents of handicapped children very much needed a few hours on a Saturday three or four weeks before Christmas to shop together free of their responsibility for their child.

After checking the church's commitment to such an idea and the suitability of their premises, the co-ordinator promised to arrange for a trained social worker to be present all day to support the voluntary helpers from the church. Although the church member responsible for the 'Fun Day' was a nurse by training, neither she nor most of her helpers had previous experience of mental handicap.

Social Services told parents about the day and the invitation was accepted for fourteen children, aged between two and sixteen.

The church arranged for forty-five people to help for all or part of the time. Each child would have his or her own minder, fourteen key people, matched to each child as far as possible from the social worker's information. These phoned or visited the child's parents in advance to learn more about the child's particular abilities, interests and needs. Some of them handed over to a second minder for the afternoon. Other people manned the exits at all times, organised games and entertainments, and provided refreshments. The day had to be a treat for the children as well as a break for their parents.

The helpers assembled in some trepidation at 9.45 a.m. for prayer and final preparations. The children were delivered at 10.30, to be cared for until 3.30. There were few problems, thanks to the careful planning, and the day passed very happily. Social Services lent toys to boost the church's own supply. They played games like Pass the Parcel and Musical Chairs, and the church youth music group entertained them, encouraging the children to join in, singing with little tune but lots of rhythmic clapping, and shaking tambourines and bells.

Several of the helpers described the day afterwards. The youngest child, a tiny girl with Down's Syndrome, was 'not much more than a baby, who looked almost doll-like. She toddled around so quietly and gently, and quite won our hearts and not a few cuddles.' The most boisterous was a boy of nine, totally deaf, 'one of the most active boys any of us had seen for a long time. He could not speak, yet his eyes spoke volumes, and he was so full of life and vitality.' Another helper defines this further: 'He was never still but leaped on to tables, on to window ledges and once straight on to the hatch and through into the kitchen.'

After five hours of looking after Susie (with a break for lunch when someone else took over) I could appreciate the strain her parents are under. Ten seconds was about the longest Susie could concentrate on anything, and that was a bottle of Coca-cola. She couldn't talk, but laughed and sometimes cried for no apparent reason. She never stood or sat still, and had an eye like a hawk for any open door which she could dart through. She loved music and marched happily around when someone was playing or singing. She wouldn't be touched or cuddled and seemed to show no response to anyone or anything except music and the Coke bottle. Yet when Susie's mother came to collect her, I found myself hoping that I could look after her again the next time.

My little boy was Stephen, aged thirteen but the height of an average eight-year-old. At first he just held my hand tightly and walked around looking at everything and greeting everyone, including me, every five minutes – 'Hello!' 'Hello, Stephen.' The book corner took his interest – he searched through the books methodically, discarding them one by one, until he finally found what he wanted – a picture of a fairground. This he brought to show me, and assured me he was going to a fair that evening, a constant hope of his . . . Every so often throughout the day he would return to that one picture.

Mark, a friend of Stephen's, was there, quite happy until he met one particular little girl, when he would scream and shout. For a change we took Mark and Stephen up into the church. They liked its size, and the flowers being arranged, but most of all a microphone. We all sat round singing nursery rhymes into the mike, Mark especially happy to hold such a coveted object, although it wasn't switched on.

When the time came for the parents to collect their children, we had mixed emotions. There was a feeling of exhausted relief that our brief period of responsibility was over, and yet sadness that the relationships which had been built up during the day were now at an end.

It gave us all a great sense of joy to be able to do this. One mother and father said the day gave them the chance of their first day out for as long as they could remember. Another mother went home to spend the day with her normal son. We expect to do it again . . .

Given time to recover, all the helpers volunteered again, and others in the church decided to join in. It is now seen as a regular activity of the church once each quarter.

Another church, this time an ecumenical one in a city centre, observes particular needs among adults who are not quite labelled, and cared for, as mentally handicapped, yet really lack the mental ability to run their lives without help. Such people can fall through the various nets of care and there are a number among the vagrant communities of most big cities. Some asked this church whether its 'drop-in' centre, open in the mornings, could extend its hours. The church is discussing the needs of these people with the Social Services to see what can be done for them.

Many city churches are concerned about people like this. Supportive friends can help some of them cope with life

much better but, although more able, they are less appealing
to work with than some of the severely handicapped children
just described.

Help them develop as people

For most churchgoers the church is, among other things, an
important source of friends. That can be especially valuable
for handicapped people living in the local community but not
always readily accepted by it.

For Richard and many others like him, it is not difficult.
Young and sweet, cheerful, clean and wholesome, they are
themselves friendly and people warm to them and think how
nice it is for them to be part of normal life. A few people shy
away, but most will meet a friendly approach with a friendly
response.

This year a change of arrangements meant that my husband and I took Richard with us to the Christian Resources
Exhibition. We need not have worried. He had a lovely time
– all those friendly Christian people with lots of interesting
things to show him. It was interesting to watch strangers'
reactions. I was not surprised to find him deep in conversation with the man from Shaftesbury Homes, or chatting
about the music to the Salvation Army officer. He enthused
to the YMCA about their national centre, recognising pictures of the place where his class had just enjoyed an adven-
ture week.

Some stallholders were a bit startled and looked round
hastily to see if he was with someone, but most tried to listen,
for he was only commenting on their displays. Some, often
women probably used to talking to young children, went to a
lot of trouble to show him things and explain their wares
intelligibly to him. He heard about work among seamen,
watched Bible stories in cartoon video, collected an assort-
ment of pens, and was encouraged to try out a computer
(familiar objects even to handicapped members of his generation). With this book in mind, I was gleeful to observe his
successful call at the stand of SPCK Worldwide. The kindly,

older gentleman in charge showed him how a card model folded into a book or a bookstall. From their conversation Richard could later tell us something of the mission's work.

We all had a good day, thanks to a lot of people who, however surprised to see him there, treated Richard with respect and made that little bit of extra effort needed to respond to him.

But what about someone like Joan? Middle aged, badly dressed, just about clean, with a funny, loud voice, she tries so hard to be normal. In one year she lost her job, her mother and her home (she had lived with her mother but the house, left jointly to her and her sister, had to be sold). Joan accepted it all without complaint or bitterness, and has settled down into a little flat. Elizabeth, a friend at church, asks her to tea sometimes, as do a couple of other families. Joan enjoys visiting, though she can be difficult with children. She keeps telling them off, because that is her experience of how children are treated. Elizabeth thinks it is a pity more of the church does not share in befriending Joan, to make it better all round.

Elizabeth once suggested that Joan might like to go on the rota for doing teas at church, but Joan declined to offer her services. Elizabeth tried to get the other ladies to invite Joan to help – and quickly realised that Joan understood better than she did. The others explained that Joan could not do that, she would put people off. When Joan, with a bundle of programmes, tried welcoming people to a function at the church, Elizabeth was asked to stop her. It is a congregation of nice, middle-class people who like everything to be done beautifully. How do you incorporate someone like Joan fully into such a church?

Maureen is not so different from Joan and her church is in middle-class suburbia, yet she is more accepted, perhaps because she is cleaner. Certain friends in the church tend to smother her with kindness, doing more for her than she needs. At least they make sure she gets to everything, but are inclined to answer for her when anyone else comes to talk. Maureen has her own little flat and loves to entertain there.

People hesitated at first to accept her invitations, but they have come to realise that it can be a pleasant and relaxing meal. Maureen knows that conversation is not her strong point, so she invites two friends at a time and settles them down for a chat while she delights to serve them.

Character development is an interactive process, not something that just happens in a vacuum. People who, whatever their intellectual limitations, find themselves valued and liked by others will respond to this. Within society today, which can get pretty self-centred, churches should be communities in which people matter for themselves, as they matter to God. The handicapped child growing up in the church needs to learn that he matters for himself, not just for his parents' sake. This will help him to move out from his parents' protective shadow. Adults who are conscious of their own inadequacies, as many handicapped people cannot help being, may not easily achieve a proper self-respect. Friends accepting them and being ready to like them as they are can make all the difference.

Some who have fair speech but difficulties in relationships like to tell tales, often greatly embroidered. Before writing them off as habitual liars, it may be worth trying to hear what they are really telling you. A story, in which either the person himself or someone else appears as a hero righting some wrong, may be his way of confessing to that wrong. He has done something that is on his conscience but is instinctively reluctant to own up for fear of losing self-respect and friends. These are not innocents, free from guile, but human sinners for whom the church has a message of forgiveness and hope.

Treating individuals with respect helps even those who are much more handicapped to grow as people. A hospital chaplain observes that a valuable side-effect of the work comes from increasing their awareness of one another. Within worship they may learn about co-operating to do things and about taking turns. It is both part of Christian loving and an aspect of behaviour which often needs to be developed. Developing mutually helpful relationships becomes very important

66

for those moving into smaller hostels and group homes.

So often these folk are made to feel they do not matter. People talk to parents or carers over their heads. Parents of sick children are sometimes cut to the quick when a doctor asks whether they want treatment, given their child's handicap. Are we sure the handicapped themselves never catch the nature of the enquiry? If Richard had had pneumonia at birth we might have been relieved to see 'nature take its course' and could have resented medical intervention if it had seemed that he was not 'meant' to live. When he developed pneumonia at two, we were horrified when the doctor asked how we felt about the full treatment. By then he had become a real person in our eyes at least. On the other hand, I was glad that the dentist saw his condition as a reason for excusing him the adolescent horrors of orthodontal treatment. Some of these attitudes, often expressed in their presence, must get through to the people concerned.

Doris has been ill recently. She is elderly and her physical condition has deteriorated, with several painful ailments. When a church friend called on her, the young care assistant was glad to let off steam. She had escorted Doris to a hospital appointment, ready to interpret and help explain as necessary, but was indignant that the doctor only addressed her. Doris was quite capable of telling him where it hurt. At the end the consultant told the carer that it was not worth trying further treatment because of Doris's mental handicap. To the young carer Doris was a real and likeable old lady, but to the doctor she hardly appeared to be a person at all.

It is easy to get indignant about this, but the church is not immune from it. That doctor is not so different from the vicar who says 'What's the point?' when parents want their handicapped baby baptised, or the Baptist minister who maintains that God loves them but says they do not understand enough to join the church.

Christians do not have a monopoly on goodwill either. Other people, surprised to encounter someone with a mental handicap out and about, often respond with natural kindness. Where someone is visibly handicapped yet clearly trying to fit in and do things properly, most people are glad to see this. Such a handicapped person is meeting them half-way, making their response easier. It is much harder to know how to treat someone whose behaviour just is peculiar. Where human instincts flounder, we may need to fall back on a greater love.

Show that God loves them

God's love for man is at the heart of the gospel: it is what the church is about, but the emphasis here is on *showing*. Most of us work mainly through words, but *telling* the gospel message is inadequate for the non-verbal, or for those whose use and understanding of words is restricted. They need to experience the church as the Body of Christ, through which they learn about God. This is true for us all, but becomes all-important when communicating the gospel to the handicapped. It may be a salutary reminder to the rest of us, perhaps especially in a denomination like mine which stresses the Ministry of the Word and shies away from mystery. It is no good sticking up pretty posters that proclaim 'God is Love', if his Body fails to bear witness to the words.

Coming from an evangelical tradition and never doubting that God loved our son, we wondered for years whether Richard could be capable of personal faith. This mattered to us; it underlay my early question, 'Will he be able to think at all?' No one offered reassurance on that, warmly though our church had taken Richard to its heart, until a friend showed me a Roman Catholic publication on the religious education of the mentally handicapped.[3]

I have rarely read a book with more excitement. On the very first page was the assertion that 'those we call mentally handicapped are capable of a life of faith.' The author, David Wilson, went on to explain that they can realise that 'I am loved – I am lovable – I am important to God.' Response to that brings the love of God into their lives and also helps their sense of personal worth. The self-confidence derived from this in turn helps them relate to others. By then we were beginning to perceive that Richard was *capable* of his own response. I might find the Catholic terminology and settings unfamiliar, yet I still found the book exciting and reassuring. To have read it back in the early days, when we had little idea of Richard's future development, would have given far more hope and encouragement than any of the published mothers' stories that friends seemed to proffer in profusion. It is so easy to assume that there is a cut-off point on the IQ scale below which people cannot understand about responding to the gospel, but love and faith do not depend on intelligence. Those who show love, beginning with the parents, can open channels for the love of God.

Any Christian education for handicapped children or adults must be backed up by their experience of the church, however restricted or extensive that may be. That must be true of all Christian education, but the responsibility of the whole church is thrown into greater relief when considering people who are more alert to atmosphere than words.

When Gordon, no longer a child, charges into church flinging his arms round all in reach with a slobbery kiss –

When Molly, who is slow and clumsy and a bit smelly, offers to help wash up –

When Tracey plonks some flowers in a vase and thinks they will beautify the church –

When Andy, whose clothes are never straight and whose remarks always end in a giggle, appears among those volunteering to deliver the magazine –

does our response help them experience the love of God?

Churches find different ways of handling these friends. There is no dogmatic answer right for every case, but you can be sure they will understand rejection all too well. They also understand when people care.

Handicapped people often know about institutional kindness and appreciate the 'extra' of the personal touch. On Richard's birthday we invited all his college class home for a party. As my husband drove some of them across south London he was fascinated to hear how many of the halls they passed had housed a party for the handicapped. Visiting a private house was a novelty.

In *House of Joy*[4] Margaret Davies, the head of a special boarding school, tells how each year a nearby church asked for a list of three things each girl would like for Christmas. The list went up at church for people to select items to send as personal gifts. A new girl, hearing of this, told another,

'I know, I've been in places where they gives out things.'
'No, you don't then,' said her friend. 'It's not like that. Your presents have your name on them and they are all sent by good friends.'
'They can't send anything to me. They don't know me.'
'Yes, they will.'
'How could they? Who tells them to do it?'
For a moment the other hesitated.
'I don't rightly know, but I reckon it's the Lord Jesus Christ.'

Holy matrimony

It is one thing to see that God's love extends to the mentally handicapped. Is it another to recognise their right to human love? For many Christians marriage is a sacrament and for the rest of us it has a special religious significance. Sometimes the church may be called on to conduct a wedding ceremony between a man and woman with mental handicap. A minister describes such a celebration:

Neil and Wendy are in their fifties and both had spent long years in traditional institutions. Neil came to us first when he moved into a purpose-built hostel near to the church. He had attended churches all his life and part of his religious history could be told by his uninhibited ability to grunt 'amens' all the way through sermon and prayers. Our church made him welcome, made sure he was collected for every kind of family event and found him small but significant jobs to do on the premises.

At the hostel Neil was placed in a community home, along with another man and two women, on the same site as all the other facilities, but detached and designed so that the four could discover how to manage for themselves many of the basic responsibilities and privileges of independence. Wendy was one of the women. Whereas Neil was vocal and could almost read, Wendy's experience of more than thirty years of institutionalisation had left her silent and apparently helpless. They appeared together each week at the handicapped club, which also meets on church premises, but nothing else was said at first.

We are assured that it was without prompting from others that one day Neil arrived at church proudly announcing that he had asked Wendy to marry him and she had accepted. Most people responded very cautiously, uncertain whether this was the sort of thing which should be 'allowed' to happen, and I, as the newly arrived minister, rather nervously arranged to spend a little time with them together. My nervousness proved totally unjustified.

I was never in any doubt from that first meeting that Neil and Wendy were genuinely 'in love' and that the experience was already bringing to both a new kind of liberation and dignity. At first Neil did all the talking, but immediately the prestige of being a 'fiancée' seemed to release new dimensions in Wendy and soon she was beginning to put more words around her experience.

It would have been very hard to follow this through if it had not been for the marvellous co-operation of all those involved in the couple's life. The warden of the hostel, the social worker and myself met and agreed a timetable and strategy for helping them through. Together we faced the almost violent opposition from Wendy's family and were able to see hostility transformed into loving support. It became clear that Wendy's potential for marriage brought into question all the decisions which the family had made on her behalf over the years – and guilt was rife. It was necessary to delay the wedding until all the parties were properly reconciled, but this did not seem to matter unduly to the couple as long as they knew that a date was fixed.

Preparation for the wedding was great fun. Several times we had to pinch ourselves and remember that it was their wedding and not ours and that there was no value in making decisions on their behalf. In the end, therefore, they chose everything from clothes to hymns and in the choosing they continued to grow. Friends inside and outside the church, their imaginations now fired, were amazingly generous and everything was done with 'nothing but the best'.

I had a new problem to work through. How much was it important to design a special service which Neil and Wendy could understand in every detail and how important was it to let their wedding be just like any other? We compromised. Almost everything was done like the royal wedding they had watched a year before. We trimmed the 'repeat after me' parts to a minimum,

71

reshaping some of the traditional wording into a question merely needing 'I will', and we shifted the legal tangle about 'just impediments' to the quietness of the vestry while signing the registers with witnesses. This simply avoided the indignity of stumbling over a difficult public performance.

The wedding itself was a delight and, I think, became something of an inspiration to the church, as well as to the many visitors who were there on the day. The congregation was swelled by all the other residents of the hostel and the whole occasion was marked by a spirit of celebration and joy. Even Wendy's family, so reluctant at first, gave themselves wholeheartedly on the day.

The wedding, of course, is only a beginning. The continuing story would not be possible but for the daily support of those who work at the hostel. I am left in no doubt, however, that Neil and Wendy have gained immensely from the whole experience, and I now hear talk of a possible bungalow away from the hostel, but still in the midst of the community. They will need support for the rest of their lives, but if it can be support rather than domination, I am sure they can continue to grow in independence and stature for a long time to come, and that church and community will be all the richer for their married presence among us.

Baptism and Holy Communion

It is one thing to have handicapped people in the worshipping congregation, but is it another to welcome them into the full sacramental fellowship of the church?

The Baptist understanding, with its stress on a personal response from the believer, may emphasise the difficulties here, but in fact all churches face similar questions. To some people it seems obvious that God's love must embrace the handicapped in a special way and they have no difficulty over the sacraments. For others there are real and difficult questions. Can godparents take baptismal vows in good faith where they doubt the baby's capacity to develop enough to make his or her own confession of faith in due course? Without baptism, can they be admitted to the Communion table? If not, most will understand that they are being excluded from a special kind of sharing together.

Baptists recognise only those two sacraments; churches

72

with more will see other implications. This is not the place to explore the theology, but it matters. If we care about handicapped people coming fully into the church, we want it done with integrity, as something felt to be right before God, not by bending the rules for kindness' sake.

A vicar describes a special baptism. Mandy was two years old and severely limited in her responses. 'Her limp figure, not unlike a rag doll, was strangely appealing.' The Harvest Festival Family Service was deliberately chosen. Mandy's family and all the staff of the home where she lived had anticipated a quiet service but were delighted at the choice of a public occasion.

> Well over a hundred people, including a lot of children, grouped around the font. There was a great sense of God's love for all his creation, especially the feeblest. The lighting of Mandy's baptismal candle seemed to demonstrate the Light of Christ in a world where much goes wrong. Many who were present remember it as an outstanding occasion in our parish life and Mandy is warmly greeted now when she is brought to our special services.

Back at the residential home there was a telling effect too. Not long before a child had died, a rare occurrence which had shaken staff and children. 'The baptism of Mandy demonstrated a hope which had something of resurrection about it. It was a particularly happy occasion for the community after the previous traumatic sadness.'

Parents may long to see their child received fully into their church, yet fear to impose on human goodwill. For this very reason they may find the subject hard to raise, even if they sense it is becoming important to their son or daughter, who has to communicate through them.

A remark in a sermon made one mother realise that confirmation might be possible for her daughter. Rather than approach the vicar direct, she rang a local radio station during a religious broadcast phone-in and asked whether it could be possible. Fortunately the crossed lines were disentangled.

How strict should be the criteria for confirmation or believer's baptism? These are matters to be taken seriously.

If exclusive arguments are advanced – 'He's just copying his friends', 'She's saying what she thinks we want to hear,' 'How can we be sure the parents know what he wants when he cannot speak?' – we need to be sure we are not applying stricter criteria to handicapped people than we would to others. I hear some Baptists say 'He wouldn't understand about taking decisions in church meetings,' which is an unfair barrier if there are abler members who do not bother to attend and take part anyway!

In the absence of clear rules, much depends on individual judgements. A mother whose Down's son wanted to be confirmed like his sister found that neither the vicar nor the rural dean knew whether confirmation was possible. She tackled the bishop when he was visiting the church and he was happy to confirm the youth on a basis of regular attendance and his clear sense of belonging to the church.

In another church a lady, who was thirty-eight although her mental age was nearer eight, attended regularly with her parents, both communicants, but had never received the sacrament herself. She was a pleasant soul, trusting and polite. To her parents' amazement, the parish priest suggested she should be confirmed. They had not imagined such a thing possible. Two simple instruction sessions were arranged, one 'theoretical', the other practical.

I can almost see some Baptists, and probably plenty of Anglicans too, writhing at this apparently casual admittance to the church. It is sobering, then, to hear the rest of that priest's story:

> After the confirmation there was a great change in her – a change which the parents couldn't get over. I am certain that Jesus is a real person to her and that a complete change came about in her through the sacrament of Confirmation and the reception of Holy Communion. If ever I had any doubts about confirming the mentally handicapped they went completely. If ever there was evidence of the Holy Spirit at work in a person it was in her. She was radiant.

Another vicar writes about Derek, widely known and loved in the parish and regularly at the altar rail with his parents to

74

receive a blessing. When he was fifteen the question of confirmation 'came persistently to the fore'.

'First we had to ascertain whether confirmation was what Derek wanted for himself and not just the wish of his parents. A lengthy course of classes would have been entirely inappropriate for him.' So that he should be at ease in familiar surroundings the bishop made a special visit to confirm him at a normal Parish Communion. A few days before, Derek was carefully rehearsed. He was given a taste of the unconsecrated contents of the chalice so that he would not be put off by something unknown. 'The opportunity was taken to explain as painstakingly as possible the difference between a consecrated and unconsecrated chalice.' At the confirmation service, Derek's mother 'made the responses with him and stood by his side as he knelt before the bishop for the laying-on of hands.' So that he should not be on his own, another adult candidate had graciously agreed to be confirmed at the same time, her husband playing for her the same part Derek's mother was playing for Derek.

It was a happy and moving occasion only marred, the vicar observed, by the church official who was heard to remark afterwards: 'How much do you suppose Derek understood about all that?'

Perhaps we can leave the matter of understanding to God. There is something lovely about the accounts of churches going to considerable trouble to ensure that confirmation or believer's baptism is a precious occasion for such candidates. So much loving care is surely something God can use in his own way.

After those reflections the next is an anticlimax. After the special, transfiguring occasions we have to return to the realities of daily life at the foot of the mount, and daily life with the mentally handicapped demands a special alertness and down-to-earth realism.

Belonging to the church is important to Bobby. He was pleased to be confirmed like his sister and impressed the congregation with his dignity on that occasion. Soon after the family went on holiday and worshipped at a church where the vicar did not like to send children away with only a word of blessing. Into each child's upraised hand at the altar he placed a Smartie. Bobby's parents knew his love of sweets and thought, 'Oh well, God will understand.' When the vicar went to give Bobby a sweet, he protested loudly, 'Don't want that. I have bread!'

For many handicapped people physically managing the communion elements can be difficult. Hospital chaplains often dip the wafer into the wine as easiest for all. One assistant remembers a visiting celebrant giving the bread first and then going round with the chalice. To the staff's amazement, everyone received the wine properly – not taking great gulps.

Churches that use little individual glasses may find some friends cannot hold these steady or drink from them. Their measure of wine can be served in a larger glass or feeding cup, set on the table with the rest and quietly handed to the deacon serving the appropriate section of the congregation.

Such quiet thoughtfulness should carry over into other communal meals. For someone whose hand shakes, half a cup of coffee may be much better than a whole one.

Decisions about admission to the sacraments and to full adult participation in the church will often lie with the clergy, but admission – inclusion – will be somewhat hollow unless the people feel it is right. It is their acceptance that ensures the handicapped member truly belongs. The whole church needs to be big enough to carry the weaker member not so much by proxy faith as in corporate faith. Then the sacraments can above all be the way in which severely handicapped people know that they truly belong to the body of Christ.

The day of Louise's baptism was wonderful, a lovely occasion. My [her minister] first real thinking about Louise came at the time of decision as to whether she should be baptised. She arrived at our church already wanting to be baptised and she and her parents asked if this could be done, although her parents took a lot of trouble to make sure I felt free to refuse. It made me think about the nature of conversion and about the highly verbal and intellectual character of our gospel preaching. Sometimes we even expect people to sign a written statement of belief. If a person cannot cope with the intellectual content of the gospel, does this mean there is no full salvation for them, no experience of God, no acceptance into the church? Of course not. So if we believe God accepts, so must we.

The next problem was to help Louise gain as much as possible from her baptism, a 'means of grace'. She and I met for preparation classes for several weeks and on some occasions I involved another of our church members with experience of mentally handicapped children. I did the best I could, but I was not very satisfied with it.

The actual baptism was a means of grace to us all. We shaped the whole service around the baptism and a member made some lovely visual aids which I used as a basis for the 'sermon', although it was largely a conversation, with Louise chipping in when she thought of something.

It was a cold day but as Louise went into the water she was quick to reassure the congregation that it was 'nice and warm'.

I am sure we all benefited from this occasion and it makes me wonder whether we ought to be more human, more sensitive, more sensual, ministering to the whole person in our worship.

5
Can They Learn about Jesus?

At school the teacher had her class writing shopping lists. Each day she chose a different kind of shop and the pupils had to write down some items they might buy there. The day she reached the fruiterer's, she was startled by Richard's list:

Oranges
Apples
Love
Joy
Peace
Bananas
Goodness
Plums. . .

'It's a good thing I'm a Christian too,' she told us gleefully, 'or I might not have seen the connection!'

Richard enjoyed his baptismal preparation classes so much that the minister felt she should continue to meet him for special study sessions, even if at monthly rather than weekly intervals. The Fruits of the Spirit seemed a possible theme on which to base a course on living as Christians today. They took the fruits one by one and found pictures and little stories to illustrate each virtue and render the concept less abstract. Some proved easier to illustrate than others but Richard was delighted with them and remains 'hooked' on the Fruits. They are one of the few things he knows by heart and he can define each one intelligibly. Whenever the passage is read in church he sits up with delight and mouths them marginally ahead of the speaker. When he observes the virtues in action he likes to name the fruit concerned, which confirms his understanding – though in some amusing contexts:

Dad, please make us some coffee: that will be kindness.
Mum and I will wait for it: that will be patience!

How realistic an aim?

People ask why the church should be concerned about Christian education for those with mental handicaps. God loves them and he will not hold their intellectual limitations against them. They remain childlike and of such is the Kingdom of God.

Yes, but . . . It is the right of every child to learn as much as he or she is able. It is a basic human right.

> Everyone has the right to education . . . Education shall be directed to the full development of the human personality and to the strengthening of respect for human rights and freedoms. It shall promote understanding, tolerance and friendship among all nations, racial and religious groups . . .[1]

Many with mental handicaps are benefiting from education in fields other than religion. Their horizons are widened, their ability to enjoy life is increased. There is a world of difference between sitting looking blank and actively leafing through a magazine, commenting now and again on something interesting.

Richard never sits around doing nothing, for he is good at occupying himself. He likes television, but will plan his viewing from the *Radio Times* and *TV Times* and is not afraid to switch off when he has had enough. Then he may listen to tapes, play father's little organ, practise snooker shots, look at books, add stamps to his collection, do some cooking, play ball in the garden, visit the library, stroll or cycle round the road to find friends to chat to . . . When he tires of such activities, it is because he is exhausted. If he flops in the armchair it is to doze off, not to stare into space.

Ah, people think, but he is 'bright', he is 'high-grade' (a horrid term which seems to be reserved for people with Down's Syndrome). Is it really just that? We remember all too vividly the toddler and the child who would so easily turn off to the world. A glazed look would settle on his face and, if allowed to 'set', he would remain awake yet almost impervious to external stimuli. You had to get in quickly to avoid this. How often someone would observe 'Richard is switching off,' and one of us, father, mother, more often than not brother, would resignedly put down some engrossing activity and do something with Richard, forcing his mind back into play. It was an effort, but the more we did with him, the more he learned to do, and the more he found to do when left to his own devices.

Keith was particularly good at adapting normal little boys' play into a teaching medium. As they crawled around the floor with their toy cars, Richard would learn to select by colour, to distinguish and eventually count and name the cars, bikes, vans and buses.

Richard was undoubtedly fortunate in having a brother willing and able to find a teaching opportunity in every game, and this must have done a lot for his range of interests. We were readier than Keith to assume that things were beyond Richard's comprehension. His brother expected that anything that appealed to him would hold some interest for Richard too.

These days many more young people with mental handicaps, well stimulated throughout childhood, are able to take a lively interest in life generally. If they are capable of learning a little, then the church should not deny them the opportunity of learning more about Jesus. To say 'God loves them and understands' can be an excuse for lack of human effort.

Religious and moral education, which deals so much with the unseen and with abstract qualities, makes particular demands on the ingenuity of the teacher. You may not be able to tackle a subject in the usual way because of the barriers of limited understanding, but approach from a fresh angle and you may find a way in. The handicapped person who is eager to learn will be delighted when something gets through. No one wants to be a failure all the time! The goal has to be realistic, but there can still be pride in achievement, which is rewarding for the teacher and good for the pupil's self-esteem.

The scope for academic education is very limited, even if more can usefully grasp the basic 'Three Rs' than was imagined a few years ago, but religious and moral education has a significant contribution to make to the 'full development of the human personality'. Learning to love one another – simply increasing awareness of one's fellows – is noted by workers with very severely handicapped people as something positive that comes from such education reduced to its simplest forms. Learning to love God is equally possible: they will not, indeed, have to wrestle with the hurdles which reason and science seem to present to some clever people. Many find comfort in a sense of God's overarching presence, and in Jesus find a friend who actually understands them. The invisibility of the risen and ascended Christ does not render him an abstraction. The idea that friends and relations can be far away yet alive and still loving is within the experience of many. This is one of the areas where the simple faith and trust of the handicapped Christian can sometimes put to shame the doubts and anxieties of the mentally able believer.

Religious awareness

This is never an easy concept to define and it is even harder when considering the mentally handicapped Christian. People in close touch with the very severely handicapped speak of restless bodies stilled for a brief spell, of rapt expressions as something gets through. A picture, or music, sometimes even a spoken word, or the very action of a sacrament, may be the trigger.

The hospital chaplain was talking about Light, and among the visual aids was a picture of a candle. Suddenly Andrew got up from his place and struggled forward. He wanted, insistently, the big candlestick from the altar. When the chaplain realised, she helped him get it and Andrew firmly held it at the front through the rest of the talk. She could not tell what, if anything, Andrew understood, for his handicap is severe, but clearly something had moved him.

Another time she asked the congregation, 'Do you talk to God during the day?' It was Andrew's voice that surprised her with its positive 'Yes!'

With rather more able people more verbal response is possible, though they may use phrases they have heard from others and it is not always easy to tell whether the thought as well as the expression is second-hand.

'How do you think about God?' another chaplain asked a group of four adults at a Training Centre. They had 'no communication problems', so were able to tell him that God is 'a nice fellow', 'someone who is very clever', 'a super father', 'a friend'. He 'helps men', 'makes us well and fit', 'helps us to help other people'. They all thought of God as being like a man. They had some sense of his creative function. One said he is 'like an artist who is upset if the creatures he made don't love him'.

Asked about Jesus, they found it hard to separate their ideas about Father and Son. Jesus is 'a kind man', 'Our Lord, who thinks of us as God does', 'not just a man but a special kind of man', 'not on earth but up there listening to our problems – wherever we go, He follows us'.

One was prepared to explain the Incarnation:

God thought the people of the Old Testament don't understand me because they cannot see me, so I will come to earth. Through Jesus all naughtiness will be forgiven. Jesus is not just human – but human and something else, because he rose from the dead. Jesus is a person who is different from everyone else – on another wavelength.

No direct question was put about the Holy Spirit but all the group of their own accord made some mention of the third person of the Trinity: 'a thoughtful ghost', 'someone invisible who stands beside me and who I cannot see'.

They knew prayer was talking to God, but

Prayer was something they only resorted to when they felt they needed help or felt that others in their immediate circle needed help. One said he did not normally pray but often thought of God. 'Do you think that gets through?' he said, 'Am I tuned in?'

Three had no regular experience of corporate worship but two liked the idea of going to church regularly if suitably introduced. The fourth had been confirmed and went either to Matins or Holy Communion each Sunday. Asked about his thoughts when 'that white circle of bread' was placed in his hands, he replied, 'Jesus is then with me.'

This group may not have been 'typical'. They had been chosen by the Centre staff as those most likely to respond in 'chat' sessions with the chaplain, but he concluded cautiously that they had retained certain religious information from past experience in home, day and Sunday school; they had a sense of the difference between God and man; they could understand in some measure the idea of a being they could not see; they showed concern for the needs of others. He judged this a basis on which a sympathetic priest or layman could lead them to a greater understanding of the Christian faith and a fuller place in the worshipping community.[2]

For those handicapped people who have been reared in the faith it can seem curiously immediate. Perhaps they are less likely than 'normal' people to pigeonhole the sacred apart from the secular. They probably have less sense of distance in time and space. Our sons returned from a walk on Epsom Downs with Keith still chuckling. Richard had read the sign over a big gateway: STABLE. 'Who lives there?' asked Keith. Richard knew that all right: 'Mary and Joseph'!

It is sometimes assumed that mentally handicapped people lack imagination but it can function, within their experience. Handicapped children probably will not take to fairy stories but prefer those that relate more or less to life as they know it. They are more likely to cope with a girl finding the porridge too hot or even a bear sitting on his suitcase at Paddington station than with witches turning princes into frogs or pumpkins into glass coaches.

David's experience includes the crib each year at his church. Christmas was well past when David, then eight, called his mother to the window where her pot plants were displayed.

'Look, crib!'
　'A crib?' asked his puzzled mother.
　'Yes. There's Baby Jesus in the manger, that's Joseph, Mary, shepherds . . .'

And mother's eye had only seen foliage there!

They may sense that something is special without really understanding it.

Megan was fifteen when she learned, in the hospital school assemblies, to sing

God is good to me,
He holds my hand,
He helps me stand,
God is good to me.

She often missed school because of behavioural difficulties, but that song stayed with her, actions and all, long after she left at nineteen. Whenever there was trouble – a tantrum, violence to another resident or member of staff, or whatever – the chaplain had only to come and sing the little ditty with her and all became calm again, relationships restored.

The chaplain just wonders why. Was it the distraction of a friend from outside? Probably, coupled with the joy of being asked to do something she *could* do. But maybe God had a hand in it somewhere.

One bedtime, when Richard was becoming aware of sounds, Keith was making him identify initials. 'What letter does *b*ath begin with?' 'B.' '*S*oap? *T*oothpaste?' and so on through the process until Keith reached, 'What does *P*rayer begin with?' 'Our Father.'

Prayer, in fact, often reveals best the religious awareness of the handicapped. Friends sometimes say to me, 'We know Richard was baptised at his own request, but how do you judge his personal faith? He says "I love Jesus", but do you have any way of knowing what that means to him?' I find the only convincing answer to that in those of his prayers we hear or overhear.

If he is anxious about someone, as when one of the family is ill, he will do anything practical he can to help and then kneel down and ask Jesus to do more. You can see he has no doubt that will have some effect.

His bedtime prayers, apart from any special intercessions, are largely a matter of thanksgiving. A happy soul, he goes back over the day telling his friend Jesus about it. On New Year's Eve his brother chanced to eavesdrop on the tail end and came down gleefully to tell us that following the final 'Amen', Richard had an afterthought: 'P.S. – A Happy New Year to you, Jesus!'

Similar observations are made by others privileged to hear the prayers of handicapped Christians. The style may be unconventional but there is a real, living quality about such friendship.

Who can teach them?

The answer is anyone who wants to *enough*.

For Christian education with the handicapped teachers do not have to have special training or qualifications, but it is not a job just anyone can be expected to undertake. Motivation – the will to tackle such work – is very important. The sort of person who teaches best may vary from church to church but they will all need to be kind, patient and keen to help them learn more. Who does best probably depends on who feels most at ease with the handicapped. Flexibility and imagination are also useful, especially when it comes to dreaming up alternative approaches, working from concepts within their experience. The skills required are similar to those needed for teaching young children, but one has constantly to bear in mind that handicapped adolescents and adults are *not* children and therefore make allowances for their age and experience of life. Language needs to be kept simple and straightforward.

Some ministers will find they can get through to these people well, while others will find it very difficult. The teacher need not be the minister, although when it comes to baptismal or confirmation classes the minister ought to be involved, even if helped by someone who has developed the necessary communication skills.

The handling of such preparation classes can be tricky, especially in their relationship to parallel ones for other, abler candidates. Simpler classes can often achieve a lot more understanding, but separate classes may stress their difference.

In some cases a happy compromise is achieved, where all the candidates meet for opening devotions and a cup of tea at the end but split into smaller groups, including one for the handicapped, for study.

In *The Unexpected Call*[3] Anne Arnott tells how her husband, a solicitor called late to ordination, visited a lady whose only child, a teenage girl, had Down's Syndrome.

> Like so many with this handicap, she was affectionate and had a real intelligence of a sort, and was anxious to learn. Mother and daughter came to church every Sunday morning, and it was plain the girl enjoyed the family Communion service . . . Tom went regularly for many weeks to prepare her for confirmation. 'She understands a great deal,' he told me, 'like what it means to be a friend of Jesus. She knows all about giving and receiving presents, and she has grasped what it means to receive the gift of love Jesus gives us, even though we don't see him. She understands about talking to Jesus, and going to the special feast of Holy Communion to which he has invited us.' So steadily and gradually he taught her something of what it means to follow Jesus, and to be loved and wanted by him. Her Confirmation was a memorable day. Her face shone with joy. I used to see her and her mother every Sunday morning afterwards, kneeling with real devotion as they remembered our Lord and received the bread and wine as from him.

In another church the minister, although sympathetic, did not feel able to tackle the main pre-confirmation teaching of a Down's girl himself. A laywoman judged to have appropriate gifts was asked to arrange a course. The minister followed the progress and joined in at various stages.

In some churches those with relevant professional backgrounds get involved with the handicapped, though it can be hard work and it is not necessarily right to do it on Sunday as well as Monday to Friday. Elsewhere other teachers may find it an interesting change. The leader of one adult Bible class is a senior teacher of modern languages on weekdays. Of her Sunday class she says:

> Compared with working in a secondary school, they are pure *joy* to teach. Their patience with those who try to teach is touching.

In school you are alert for trouble if, for example, you drop a book. This class simply tells you not to worry and waits till you are ready. Once we were trying to illustrate possible results of quarrels and deliberately knocked over a jar of water. The point was lost as there was a mad rush to the door for a cloth. They are usually eager to help. They have little sense of feeling sorry for themselves: they all know people worse off and count their blessings. Their faith is real, and it is a privilege to hear some of them pray.

Elsewhere again the teachers' backgrounds are varied and not apparently relevant: a barrister, a young mother, an office secretary. All these are making special provision for groups of mentally handicapped people. The range is wide indeed when you add in all those Sunday school teachers who successfully integrate a handicapped child with the more able in their classes and teach them quite a lot.

I used to be in a happy Sunday school class with several other girls just at the grammar school, one who had narrowly missed 'eleven plus' selection, and one from the educationally subnormal school. She was a year or two older than the rest of us and able to read slowly and laboriously. The teacher had had only elementary education before going to work as a mill girl, but she was a dear Christian to whom we all responded. From this teacher we all learned a lot, including a love of the Bible and a respect for our struggling friend, with more idea of when to prompt and when to wait for her to get there alone.

In one American church an older married couple with long experience in Christian education, have built up over the past fourteen years a large Sunday class for severely handicapped children, including twenty-five 'profoundly retarded, multiple handicapped' from a local home. 'There is clanking and clanging, humming and singing and much happy groaning' for Jesus in their worship. 'Professionals say Naomi and Cliff are unusually gifted in communicating with the handicapped.'[4]

Those working in this field also need the grace to be content with slow and modest achievements. Often they will have to be satisfied with a vague feeling that something of the spirit has got through. It is unrealistic to look for intellectual understanding, but activities in which the handicapped can participate help them feel part of the fellowship.

A school for the profoundly handicapped on a hospital compound had some eighteen pupils. The hospital chaplain befriended the staff and was eventually invited to take weekly assemblies. As most pupils lacked speech and few had full mobility, he decided to work through music and movement.

The song 'Jesus, Jesus loves _____, yes, he does, yes, he does,' sung with each one in turn with physical contact and their own names inserted became the hallmark of the times together. With some one could dance, or jump for joy, with others just getting a finger into a tiny arthritic fist and a smile in response was a triumph. Round the room we went, eighteen times, eighteen meeting points.

One day a student teacher was present, playing the piano with all the secular songs like 'Miss Polly had a dolly' and 'Six fat sausages sizzling in the pan'. A good time was had by all – almost all. Paul, aged sixteen, was sobbing his heart out. He had to be led away to his own room, with his own teacher patiently trying to find out what was wrong. Eventually Paul conveyed 'We didn't sing Jesus.' The chaplain had to be sent for and he had to sit Paul on his knee and sing 'Jesus, Jesus loves Paul, yes, he does . . .' before Paul could relax again.

Don't draw any elaborate morals from this; love comes in little things anyway. But the chaplain felt ten foot tall and all the months at eighteen choruses a week were at last worth it. Paul didn't understand, but he knew he was loved.

Patsy is very different from Paul. She is in her fifties and fairly able. A keen Bible reader, she joins in the Bible study. There she will suddenly come out with questions bothering her from her set passage several days earlier, in the midst of something quite different. 'What's the Urim and Thummim?' she demands, because she really wants to know and here surely are friends who could help. Can they manage a satisfactory answer in terms Patsy can follow?

There are no hard and fast rules about who will make good teachers of the mentally handicapped in the church context.

It might be a good guide to see who responds warmly to some of the examples given here.

How to go about it

With the young and the most severely handicapped, it is often a matter of getting them involved. A simple hymn with a catchy tune to sing or hum or clap, visual aids, pictures, puppets, mime, these all demand some response and are better than teaching all in words.

A chaplain taking a hospital service took as the theme one week 'Hearing God,' using Elijah's story, and they had great fun with the sound effects. Members of the congregation blew into the microphone to make the rushing wind. They all rocked to the earthquake, with the organ joining in (but with care not to over-excite them). Everybody waved crêpe paper flame streamers. Then, in contrast, came the still, small voice. They all enjoyed chapel that morning. One or two will have caught at something more about God.

That kind of effort would hardly be part of regular worship in the local church, but some participatory element is not uncommon and it may be used to draw any handicapped people present more into the act of worship.

People who attempt Christian education with older and more able mentally handicapped people – teenagers and adults – quickly discover that there is hardly any suitable published material. Again and again they have to adapt and to produce their own, which considerably adds to the time-consuming demands of such work.

There is plenty of material for use with children and much of this can be used with handicapped children rather older than it is basically intended for, but it is rarely suitable for those beyond childhood. The concepts and language levels may still be appropriate but the pictures and settings are childish. Children's Bibles and Bible storybooks can often be used, but there is a lack of suitable books, especially material relating Bible teaching to life today. Churches remind us from their experience that this may need to include matters of sexual morality and attitudes to the occult. The handicapped are part of today's world.

Around the country there must be a number of people putting their own lessons together, some in well-structured courses, but much of this is done in isolation and there is little sharing of ideas. One understands the religious publishers' need for viable markets and this one exists in little pockets, not easily identified as a whole, but certainly growing.

'Got any books for me?' continues to be asked wistfully at a number of church bookstalls. Books and magazines are wanted by handicapped adults themselves, not only by their teachers.

There is particular need for courses preparing for confirmation or believer's baptism. First a church has to decide that admission to the sacrament is appropriate – and a recent survey of Baptist churches shows a divergence of opinion on the principle which would probably be echoed in most denominations:

> 'For severely handicapped people these things have no relevance.'

> 'They should be loved and made to feel wanted but I cannot see the point in offering membership to a person who is incapable of understanding what it is about.'

> 'The sacraments are God's gift to us and, in certain circumstances, to give baptism and communion to those severely handicapped is to take the step of faith and say "God loves you – you are valued and cared for by God".'

> 'We would in effect be saying, "Yes, you are part of our life". The sacraments are a way of saying what is beyond the capacity of all of us to express in words.'

Where the church decides that admission is right, many now feel they ought to take preparation as seriously as for other candidates – but how to go about it?

One minister suggests helping them understand the significance of symbols, beginning with the familiar handshake, hug or kiss, and thinking about what was being offered and received.

Speech problems are common among handicapped people and often leave would-be friends at a loss. Because Anna's handicap is not mental, she is more able to convey what it feels like to have major difficulty with communication. She helped her minister write this account to help others understand.

Anna is a pupil at the residential school for the physically handicapped close to the church. She shares with many who are physically and/or mentally handicapped, difficulties of verbal communication. When Anna was fifteen, she requested Believer's Baptism. She was patently sincere and one's inclination was to baptise her, but what of preparation? At the suggestion of the school's staff we had an extended period of 'one-to-one' preparation. From the beginning, Anna and I agreed that problems of understanding would be faced without embarrassment. Progress might be slow sometimes, but I wouldn't deceive her that I had understood her when I hadn't. In practice, with practice, understanding was not as difficult as might have been expected . . . Her revelations about her faith were an inspiration and in common with other candidates Anna gave verbal testimony in the service before being baptised. This was accomplished by questions and answers prepared beforehand for an interview on the day. Anna's speech therapist, a Christian, was present and was very gratified. Anna is ambulant and baptism by total immersion created no practical difficulties. But Anna's relationship with the church is a continuing one. She needs a listening ear; she has questions and problems like any teenager. Unfortunately when people cannot readily understand distorted speech they feel embarrassed, they offer 'yes' and 'no' answers hoping they are appropriate, they avoid entering into conversation or, at best, do not listen for long. Certainly the person with handicaps is underestimated and undervalued.

Talking to Anna has revealed some of the inner feelings of a person with handicaps. Unlike her, many cannot easily express their feelings, and perhaps aren't given the opportunity beyond 'Do you take sugar?' Anna tells me that she wants to be treated normally. The school has done much to equip her for life. Sign language, word charts, phrase books and computer technology are employed, though she would hope to talk, normally. Like Anna, many people with handicaps face moves, with new relationships to form, new people to develop those skills of communication with all over again!

Instruction sessions may be reduced to one or two, largely going through what actually happens in the service, or extended over several months. It depends on the individual's ability. Few will be able to concentrate for long at a time but the more able, like Richard, will value the learning process and can gradually absorb quite a lot of teaching, provided it comes in small doses. Our minister found she could deal with many of the key concepts, simplified from her usual young people's baptismal course, but she could only introduce one a week, rather than tackling several in one session. Since Richard enjoyed the lessons and subsequently retained much of what he learned, it seemed right to take a year over it.

Some will welcome a little simple homework to keep the subject alive between sessions. Homework may, in fact, be dignifying in itself, if it is a dominant feature of teenage brothers' and sisters' home life, usually omitted from special education! Richard enjoyed looking for pictures to illustrate the current theme (and it proved a useful way of discovering how much he had understood), so a topic was often begun one week and completed the next, a form of revision, before moving to the new theme.

In another church Alan could prepare for the forthcoming lesson, using notes his minister prepared and looking up Bible references at his own pace, so that when they met the minister was developing ideas not completely new to Alan. The church treated Alan's baptism as a celebration of his new birth. He knew about birthdays so they made it a special one, with a party tea afterwards. 'One friend had made a beautifully iced cake in the form of an open Bible and many members of the congregation gave Alan a small present. The end result was a service very different from normal but very meaningful for Alan and very moving for those who know and love him.'

Elsewhere Stephen, an eighteen-year-old with Down's Syndrome, joined the normal baptismal class, mostly rather younger, and this was clearly right for him, even if he could not understand every word. He was used to being among the church's other young people and in the Boys' Brigade, so knew he belonged among them. In such a group good material with plenty of pictures and not too much solid reading would probably increase the amount understood by the handicapped candidate and be enjoyed by all.

Richard and others like him have enjoyed compiling a scrapbook of their lesson material. Loose-leaf binders or the photograph albums with acetate page covers provide sturdy protection for collections likely to be heavily used. They also enable work to be 'got right' before insertion (a handicapped candidate may like to do some writing himself but not always be able to read the result easily, so getting the page 'right' is not just being fussy over spelling and grammar). Such books can include pictures of Bible stories, paintings of Jesus (Richard and I had an interesting visit to the National Gallery to look for some of these), photographs of the local church and its activities, little stories about modern Christians, prayers etc. Richard particularly enjoyed some sessions on the different kinds of prayer: from 'thank you' prayers (including a startling one for the joy of rhubarb crumble and thick custard!) to intercession for people known and for others seen to need help in pictures from the week's newspapers.

Such home-made books can be tailor-made for the individual. They can be looked at again and again, reinforcing the teaching, and they can be shown to friends.

> For a while Mandy carried her book everywhere. Her school became interested and she added some work there. She read it to all her friends – she certainly did her part in sharing the gospel!

Mandy's church found a further spin-off. Having taken photos to illustrate their church life for her, they put duplicates in a second album to take to show housebound members.

'Friends of Jesus' is a useful title for linking New Testament and modern Christians. Richard enjoyed collecting photos of people working for his church: the minister preaching, the organist playing, the lady arranging flowers, people doing running repairs and cleaning, people serving teas and so on. Among these he was able to include some of himself also sharing helpfully in the life of the church, giving out hymn books and collecting empty coffee cups. For him these pictures speak of a fellowship of friends, a family to which he belongs.

Ernest Bladon[5] suggests a helpful outline for a course for mentally handicapped adults, 'an experiment in extending human emotions and feelings into religious concepts':

SESSION 1 Getting to know you ⎫
SESSION 2 Getting to know me ⎭ (Fellowship)

SESSION 3 Questions – Problems. Where do we find the answers? – parents, friends – those who care.
(God cares)

SESSION 4 Words – Talking – Conversation – Telephone – two way.
(Talking with God – Prayer)

SESSION 5 Gifts – birthdays, Christmas – Give and take – sharing – a sign of love.
(God so loved the world that he gave . . .)

SESSION 6 Nice things – happiness, kindness, friendship, good manners.
(Be ye thankful)

SESSION 7 Nasty things – anger, lying, cheating, jealousy.
(Forgive one another as God forgives you)

SESSION 8 This way or that way? Road signs – going in the right direction – need for a guide.
(I am the Way, the Truth, and the Light)

SESSION 9 Relations/hips – Father/Mother – son/daughter – brother/sister – Family
(The Family of God)

SESSION 10 Fan Club – someone to copy (dress, speech, manners) – someone to follow. 'I like what he does.'
(Jesus said 'Follow me')

Religious education for the mentally handicapped may sound daunting but it can be worth trying. Experience suggests that it can be rewarding for student and teacher alike. It is interesting how many able people find their own understanding refreshed by the need to get away from abstract concepts and the familiar churchy language.

This getting down to basics and relating key concepts to real life experience applies both to separate and integrated teaching. Either way the handicapped person is likely to appreciate the special effort made to take him or her seriously, as someone who also matters.

Teaching about death

This may surprise some as an area of concern on which to focus, but we hear from all angles that the mentally handicapped are poorly served here. The surprise is probably because we instinctively want to protect them from harsh reality and we hope that lesser understanding will save them from the sharper emotions. It does not. If we find thoughts of death mysterious and frightening, so do they. We all mourn the loss of loved ones. For the handicapped, whose social circle is often very small, the death of a parent or friend makes a massive impact on their little world, the more bewildering because it is harder, often impossible, for them to talk about their feelings. They are often ill-prepared for death simply because it is hard for them to grasp anything beyond their previous experience.

Of Mencap's various striking posters the most telling for me was that which ran: 'No sense, no feeling? They may not think as clearly but they feel as deeply.'

This is clearly a matter about which the church should care.

Today's handicapped people know about violence and death: they watch television like the rest of us, but the box does not impinge on our feelings in the same way as personal experience.

The girls from a special boarding school were taken to

church, where the Bible stories were new to most, as their interest showed.

> On Palm Sunday the matron found Donna crying bitterly. 'What is it? Is your ear bad again?'
> 'No, not my ear. It's what Miss said this morning – about the Lord Jesus. They didn't really do it, did they? Not kill him like that – they couldn't have. He was so kind. He didn't do any harm to anyone. Oh, say it wasn't true.'[6]

People without Donna's ability to communicate will also find the death of someone they love hard to believe. A father writes about his severely autistic son who had lived in a hospital from the age of nine but returned home each weekend. The mother had a sudden severe stroke and died in mid December. Nicholas was then in his mid-teens but they could not communicate with him enough to tell him of his mother's death. His sister, a college student,

> insisted that Nicholas should be brought home for Christmas as we always had done. When he came home expecting to be greeted by his mother he searched each room, cried in anguish and started to throw the furniture around. We tried medication and consolation but eventually had to return him to hospital on Christmas Day. Since then he has only been home on one occasion to stay and this again met with no success.

Quite often handicapped children are born to older parents and this, coupled with the longer time many live at home with parents, means they are actually more likely than other young people to lose a parent who is still very much a part of their daily life.

These vulnerable people need some preparation for the death of someone dear to them. It should include an introduction to the strangeness of funeral practice and somehow convey a note of Christian hope. An example of how this was handled off the cuff within one family comes from Ann's sister:

> It was Easter Day and Ann, home for the weekend, attended the local Baptist church with her family. Her ability to understand was very limited indeed. At the front of the church was a beautiful cross of white flowers.

Ann: 'See that cross?'
Sister: 'Yes'.
Ann: 'Mr X had one like that on his box. Why?'
Sister: 'Do you like it?'
Ann: 'Yes.'
Sister: 'We all have a cross like that when we die and meet Jesus. In fact we cannot have one like that until we do meet Jesus.'
Ann: 'What's the box for?'
Sister: 'Well, what do we do with an old coat?'
Ann: 'Throw it away – put it in the dustbin?'
Sister: 'Well, the box is a sort of special dustbin, because when we meet Jesus we have a new body and we don't need the old one.'

This may not be a very theological explanation, but it was an attempt to explain the Christian hope of resurrection. Most of us, if we are honest, need the reassurance of this hope at times of bereavement. Why should we expect mentally handicapped men and women to be different?

That conversation, and especially the cross of flowers, was remembered helpfully when Ann's father died soon after. Ann was encouraged to take an interest in Dad's box and his lovely flowers. She attended the funeral and helped with the mourners' tea. She was not left out on the edge of the family circle.

George is in his early twenties. He comes from a large, deprived family with three handicapped members. After his mother's death some years ago the eldest girl tried to keep house for the chronic invalid father and her brothers and sisters. The house was appalling: newspapers on the floor, one bed and one blanket. George was greatly at risk wandering the streets at night. Eventually he was put on probation for setting off all the fire alarms he could find. Having gone into a local authority hostel, he became cleaner, better fed, more cheerful and chatty. In every way things seemed better.

Last year his father died. One would expect him to have become less attached to this man who had done so little for him. But on a residential weekend with the Bible class seven months later George's grief and loss were intense and much of the weekend was spent with him in tears. Until then he had been given little chance to show his emotion. His grief was acute. It taught us that outward and visible signs of being well cared for tell us little of the inner mind.

One of the older residents at a home for mentally handicap-ped children died. She had been a particular favourite of a more able resident and they had a good relationship. Moira was devastated by her friend's death. All the group went with the staff to the funeral. The superintendent recalls:

> We had a very emotional scene at the grave side when Moira wanted to try to get on top of the coffin to comfort her friend. I personally had to talk through the whole situation with her and we were much later than the rest to leave.
>
> Moira's knowledge and belief of God and Jesus was very simple but very moving. She had recently been confirmed in the Church of England (her own choice) and the local non-stipendiary priest spent some considerable time going through the confirmation with her.

The Christian teaching could not suppress her grief, but it gave the superintendent something to build on as he sought to comfort her.

Even where careful preparation is attempted, not all the message will get through. When a trainee at one Centre died, all her friends attended the funeral, sitting reverently as they waited and standing as the cortège entered the church.

> David had been told that he was going to Hilda's service because she had gone to Heaven. As the congregation prepared for prayer, David in a loud 'whisper' said 'Look at all the pretty flowers – but where's Hilda?'

In 1981 the King's Fund Bereavement Group issued a paper, *The Right to Grieve*, and some of the questions raised there were further discussed by Maureen Oswin in *Bereavement and Mentally Handicapped People*[7]. She stresses that there is no reason to think that mentally handicapped people will not experience the stages of mourning much like everyone else, and they too need special support at this time. She illustrates this with Jane's experience.

Jane lived at home with elderly parents and attended the Adult Training Centre. In both situations she could com-municate quite well although she did not use a standard signing system. After a long illness, when Jane helped care for him, her father died. Jane saw him in the coffin, went to the funeral and helped prepare the mourners' meal. Her mother told her Dad was safe with Jesus. Back at the ATC, tearful but brave, warmed by her friends' sympathy, Jane painted pictures of his death, made a pottery vase for the grave, and the drama class acted going to funerals. At home she and her mother helped each other to come to terms with their loss. For a few months Jane suffered bouts of depression, but gradually she settled back to a quiet, secure life.

Two years later her mother had a sudden fatal heart attack while Jane was at the Centre. The social worker collected a case of clothes for her but did not take Jane home for fear of upsetting her. Instead she was whipped off to a strange hospital twenty miles away. A distant relative arranged the funeral and did not think it appropriate for Jane to attend. Poor Jane, her happy life shattered and having great difficulty in communicating with strangers, however well-meaning, became anxious, quarrelsome, and even aggressive. Concerned visitors from her old ATC were told they disturbed her, for she wept when they spoke of her mother. Eventually Jane settled down, but to a more withdrawn and passive life.

Anyone pastorally involved with mentally handicapped people needs to recognise that mourning will sooner or later be part of their lives and that the Christian hope is for them too.

In one of the L'Arche community homes there was anxiety on the part of the not-so-handicapped at the impending death of one of the community members. How would they all take it?

When the event took place it felt right to hold prayers around the bed. Though it was made clear that no one had to, everybody did come. The chaplain prayed and they all sang a simple song together, 'Jesus loves me' (remember the last verse?).

Later when the body was put in the ambulance they were all there on the front step, waving it off: 'Bye bye, Johnny, see you in heaven!'

Why try to teach them?

The answers to How? and Who? have tried to show the value

there can be in helping those with moderate, severe, and even profound learning difficulties to know more of Jesus.

For some it will not really go beyond the comfort of 'folk religion' – but that in itself is something plenty of more able people rely on. The hospital chaplain sees this reassurance sought when residents take her hand and lay it on their heads, wanting her to bless them, wherever they happen to meet. They associate her with church and it has a comforting connotation.

The warden of a hostel attached to a special school had great difficulty to settle one boy at night when he was staying there midweek. He persisted in getting up, wandering around and pulling other boys out of bed. It took quite heavy medication to settle him at all. At home there were no such problems.

The warden again checked through the familiar home routines with his mother to see if anything was being missed out. Eventually the mother hesitantly mentioned that she always said the Lord's Prayer with him at bedtime. The warden, herself a Roman Catholic, realised the boy had indeed sometimes said a word or two from the prayer, but she had missed the message. She found that if they said the prayer together last thing the boy would not get up again, even though he might lie awake talking to himself for some time. Clearly the formula was soothing, associated with love and security, and it was something any member of staff would do easily – once they knew. Soon they found no medication at all was necessary. The warden wonders whether other parents might be sheepish to list such an item in their child's routine, not knowing whether the staff were Christian and not realising how important it had become to that child.

At the other end of the scale are those like Richard who love their Bible and really know a lot of its stories with a vivid immediacy that can associate Zacchaeus with the climbable tree over there or the Nativity with the Derby stable. This is not something far away and long ago but part of their lives. With their intuitive responses they may be quicker than most of us to see the features of their living Lord reflected on the faces of friends who, with them, make up the continuing Body of Christ on earth today.

Feeding such lambs, helping them to know more of Jesus, may not be a daunting chore with constrained objectives but a great privilege. If their childlike qualities help them to be not so much 'holy innocents' as 'pure in heart', then maybe they can see our God. Perhaps if we get close enough we too may catch a glimpse of the Lord through them.

6
What Can They Do for The Church?

Richard went with us to a big meeting of London Baptists. As a member of the host church he enjoyed welcoming people, helping to serve refreshments, directing folk to toilets, and chatting to friends old and new. Although the service was long he enjoyed it, chiefly for the exhilaration of massed hymn-singing.

Afterwards, while his father and I talked to friends, Richard helped the stewards tidy up. He hurried to put away the microphones: our amplification system was stolen last year so he deemed that a priority. Various papers had been distributed and a fair number jettisoned around the pews. That cleared, the visiting stewards departed but Richard felt his church was still untidy. The furniture of the large pulpit platform and communion rostrum below had all been moved around. The caretaker would have dealt with this next day but Richard likes to see the church in good order to the glory of God, so he set about rearranging the heavy furniture.

We were surprised when he did not join us in the church hall and eventually I went to look for him. He was standing quietly just inside the tidy chapel, with most of the lights off.

'Come on, Richard, there's no more for you to do here!'

'I can't leave yet,' he replied. 'I've no key to lock up and there's a scruffy old man in the porch. I stayed to look after the church.'

Sure enough, one of the city's vagrant population was sheltering in the vestibule. Although the church makes such folk welcome when open, we clear the building on locking up. Someone lying in a pew could be overlooked. On Sundays, as Richard knows, the chapel is locked as soon as it is empty, but that night no one with a key had appeared at the right time. The system had slipped. So Richard quietly stood guard, a responsible doorkeeper in the House of the Lord.

Accepting their gifts

When Christians think about handicapped people it is usually with compassion. We have no doubt that God loves them. We recognise that we should be concerned for them and do what we can to help them. We often liken them to the poor and outcast in the Bible. We are less ready to recognise that they may themselves have something to give. As one minister wrote, about the theoretical possibility of having a mentally handicapped church member,

> It would be understood that such a person would not be an active member, but would be the recipient of love and affection and not barred from being a member of the Body of Christ.

Handicapped people can be more than the recipients of kindness. With patient help and encouragement many can take an active and useful part in the life of the church. We 'whole' people are not very good at grasping this where the handicap is physical. We find it even harder when we meet severely restricted intelligence. It requires grace to make the leap from pity to appreciation.

Some churches have done this. They wax enthusiastic about the contribution of the handicapped people in their midst, even if rueful honesty admits to occasional embarrassments, like 'Dolly is a dear soul and we know she can't help the kleptomania. We just have to be alert, especially on church outings.' Mental handicap often demands just such down-to-earth realism hand-in-hand with noble sentiments. That will not be alien to our Lord who noticed and cared when people were hungry or had dusty feet.

Another minister, also asked about having handicapped people in the church, observed:

> The Kingdom is not about understanding, but accepting Christ's love and giving love. That is an area where many mentally handicapped people put other Christians to shame.

And one of the things most of us find hardest to accept from our handicapped friends is their instinct to embrace, their need to express affection physically. So often we find that too much, wriggling out of their arms, disturbed and embarrassed, rebuffing their friendship.

Sometimes people with mental handicaps will surprise us with what they can do. We think carefully about what is suitable and possible for them, what we can let them do. We suggest simple, menial tasks and they rejoice to do these to the glory of God and to help other people. Occasionally they decide to branch out and startle us by making a success of something we would never have thought of for them. Christ may be calling us all to see beyond the obvious! We need to be open to receive their gifts, both for what it means to them *and* because the church can benefit from them.

There is in circulation, source unknown, a set of beatitudes relating to mental handicap. They contain some telling reflections, like

> Blessed are you who ask for our help,
> For our greatest need is to be needed.

This was understood by the church which took particular care over preparing Mandy for confirmation. They even managed to incorporate it into the sacrament:

> It is our custom to have home-made bread for communion, and also for the confirmation candidates to offer the communion elements with the collection at the communion service. Mandy helped to make the bread on that occasion, so at her confirmation she carried in the bread she had made, offering it to the minister. The event is recorded in her beloved book of 'Friends of Jesus'. The public action certainly made a statement to the whole church about Mandy's ability to give as well as receive.

The gifts they bring

A term sometimes used of the mentally handicapped, usually with pejorative connotation, is 'simple-minded'. Much of what they offer to the church springs from their simplicity, so we need to be more appreciative of their simple minds.

One of Richard's friends, cruelly stunted in body as well as mind, is a radiant little soul. 'You look nice! Ooh, you look nice!' she greets her friends. 'What a nice house! What lovely food! Isn't this fun!' She sets about appreciating what life offers her, when we might think it had given her a raw deal.

Some mentally handicapped people are sad and withdrawn, fearful of the world and how it will mistreat them next. Many, by the very nature of their handicap, cannot relate to others easily or at all. By comparison those with Down's Syndrome, often happy and sociable, are blessed indeed; although, contrary to popular opinion, not all Down's are cheerful extroverts.

Nevertheless, there are plenty with mental handicaps who do not mope around, prisoners of their condition, but venture into life with spontaneity and trust. Unsophisticated, they take pleasure in simple things. They are uninhibited, and that has its delightful, as well as its embarrassing, side.

Molly lives in a hospital. She enjoys church, always saying 'Praise him, praise him!' as she enters the chapel. She loves the chaplain, whom she greets with a hug, 'Good morning, church!' The trouble is, when they go out Molly is apt to hug any large grey man as 'church'!

Molly has a passion for hats. After the bishop's visit, she was found parading the hospital grounds, a pair of pants inverted on her head, mitre-like, intoning solemnly, 'Praise the Lord!'

At our new minister's induction service the soloist was Rodney Macann, Baptist and opera singer, then appearing at Covent Garden. Richard enjoyed the solos and afterwards sought Rodney out to tell him, with simple appreciation, 'You've got a good voice!'

If Richard appears a lot in these pages it is because I am often there to witness and take note of his doings. Relatively able in many ways, yet with severe learning difficulties, he is not untypical of the semi-independent mentally handicapped people most likely to be active in churches prepared to make room for them.

Richard certainly caught the joy of Easter. Both our sons went out separately on the Saturday. Keith returned chuckling. As he came home he could hear his brother's voice drifting across from the next parallel road, uplifted in his own inimitable Hallelujah Chorus. Gradually one gets thick-skinned about what the neighbours think!

Mary was a regular worshipper, well known to most of the congregation at her church. One always knew if she was present because her Amens at the end of prayers were always late and, deliberately, loud.

One Sunday morning, prior to Christmas, at the communion service, the door suddenly opened and Mary walked in, looking for her particular friend. Finding she was not there, Mary tried to hand her bundle of Christmas cards to one of the deacons for distribution. Minister and deacons literally had their hands full just then, but one of the choir stepped forward to take the cards and assure Mary that they would be given out as requested. The conversation was conducted in a whisper by the chorister but in a normal voice by Mary, so everyone present was left in no doubt about the purpose of her visit.

A member of the congregation remarked afterwards that it needed someone as uninhibited as Mary to jolt us out of our complacency and take us down a peg or two.

Mary's effort, even if disturbing to the service, was solely in the cause of good fellowship: she only wanted to greet her various friends in the church at the happy season.

Often handicapped people have a curious discernment in personal relationships. They are quick to distinguish between the authentic or the sham. Sometimes they will get on well with apparently unlikely people, probably because they feel through outer appearances and encounter the person beneath.

'I don't know what to make of that man,' an old lady said to me, speaking of one of our deacons. 'He looks so stern, I've never seen him smile.' I knew what she meant, although I also know that he is serious rather than severe. Richard has never been put off by this and gets on well with him. I also recall that, apart from our closest friends, he was the first to include Richard specifically in invitations, for private party or sponsored walk, and this must in turn have made others think of including Richard.

We have known Richard avoid someone who is clearly making great efforts to be nice to him, enthusing about Richard's things in simple language. Do they try too hard, so that there is an artificial ring to it?

Others who always speak in long and learned words and are ill at ease with children seem to get on with Richard and he views them as friends. Maybe the very lack of allowances they make appeals to him. In the service of the church they meet and work together, man to man.

The trust handicapped people place in their friends can be demanding at times. If they feel let down, they will be hurt, and it is not easy for them to explain or take in explanations.

Jack's church has a cleaning rota in which most able-bodied members share. Jack was eager to join in, so Sylvia invited him to help her. With so many volunteers, a turn only came round at ten-weekly intervals, a long wait for Jack. 'Is it soon? Is it soon?' he asked. He did not understand dates, but grasped that their next turn would be on Easter Saturday. 'I will come,' he promised. On the day Sylvia went to the church but there was no sign of Jack. She did not worry as Jack regularly went about the village on his own, and assumed something else had cropped up.

Next day he was really cross with her. 'You let me down. You didn't come for me.' Sylvia had fetched him on a previous occasion, but the hostel was close to the church and he came on his own on Sundays. She had thought his 'I will come' meant that he would come by himself. Verbal explanations were hopeless: Jack could understand and answer but knew he could never win an argument. Instead he told Sylvia pointedly what he had done instead. She realised well enough how hurt he was.

There is a childlike quality about many of these simple souls, often seen in the pleasure they derive from birthdays celebrated with glee far into adulthood. They may be as receptive as anyone else to beauty, can appreciate pleasant surroundings and have their own personal tastes in music and art.

Crossing Waterloo Bridge one evening, we all enjoyed the

view of floodlit buildings reflected in the Thames. 'Dull would he be of soul who could pass by . . .' Richard may be dull of brain but not of soul. He exclaimed:

'Isn't it lovely? It's just like Golden Jerusalem!'

Redefining our values

Christians sympathetic to those with mental handicaps sometimes assert that they bear a prophetic witness in our materialistic, go-getting age. They take life slowly and gently, affected little by money but much by kindness and love.

I feel this is more likely to be said by those who nobly choose to work with them than by parents landed involuntarily with a handicapped child. Parents have to cope with the disappointments, problems and frustrations day in day out largely on their own. We are too busy keeping an eagle eye on our marauding, school-age toddlers, too weary from nocturnal disturbances, too anxious about our peculiar responsibility as the teenager struggles for independence, too worried about the future when we are no longer around to love and protect. We rarely stand back and see them as prophets.

Yet there is something in their representing a different set of values that may give us pause and make us see things from fresh angles. When Richard was small, I felt I could scream at the next person to coo at us, 'Aah, they bring their own love with them.' When he came of age recently, I looked at the fifty-nine birthday cards displayed on our wall – and wondered! Mind you, I might be tempted to ask whether it was naive innocence or a baser acquisitive instinct that made him tell so many friends well in advance precisely when he would be eighteen!

It rings true, though, when a church writes:

We have learned much about ourselves and been set free from many 'hang-ups' by having mentally handicapped people in our fellowship.

It is a pity they did not spell out some examples of the hang-ups from which they were liberated.

Certainly life with someone like my son teaches one to be

sparing in one's embarrassment. A friend told me recently how red in the face he and his wife had been at the remarks of an elderly, deaf relative whom they were looking after at a family wedding. I realised with wry amusement how unperturbing it sounded to me. We have had to learn to stop blushing and laugh, and save our embarrassment for worse occasions.

There is a certain blunt honesty about these people. They make it clear if they like or dislike something. They are not usually into polite cover-ups. I suppose that is rather like small children. Richard has probably never embarrassed me worse than my sister once did my mother, when she went to a birthday party and told her hostess: 'I don't like your party. I don't like your food. I don't like the other children. I don't like the games. I want to go home!' But then Richard would find that far too long a speech so his objections, although clear, would be less explicit.

They respond to kindness and friendship in an uncomplicated way. The trouble is, as has already been observed, they express this in physical embraces which often are embarrassing, especially to undemonstrative English men. 'Keep your arms to yourself, Richard,' we say. 'Gentlemen *shake* hands.' He tries to remember, but it is unnatural to him. Before long, in his pleasure at a friendly greeting, the arms are around another shoulder. It is doubtless we sophisticated folk who make life complicated, but if society lives with inhibitions it is bound to find the uninhibited uncomfortable and disconcerting.

New insights

Where people are making the effort to attempt Christian teaching of the mentally handicapped, they find it rewarding beyond immediate expectations. The lady primarily responsible for Mandy's confirmation classes observes:

> Mandy did a lot for me – I was constantly challenged to think what was the essence of the gospel in simple words – and others in the church would agree that they have been challenged in various ways.

The minister who prepared Richard for baptism found it refreshing to be forced to take such a new look at her regular course for young people. She felt that experience with Richard would lead to some new approaches and insights with the next able candidates. Reducing something to essentials is often a useful exercise in sorting out what matters most. Another teenager may want to discuss peripheral matters. With a handicapped candidate there will not be the argument: the challenge is to convey key teaching in a way that means something.

For me, and for a good many others, the 'prophetic' witness of the mentally handicapped centres on the light they throw on the importance of the Church as the Body of Christ. Perhaps other branches of the Church are more keenly aware of this understanding than most Baptists, with their stress on the gathered community of believers and on the authority of Scripture. When faced with people on whom the Ministry of the Word has little impact, whose ability to search the Scriptures to seek Christ is severely curtailed, we are forced to recognise that what is left is the Church itself. If our handicapped friends are to encounter Jesus, it will be here. It is what they see in the gathered community – or in any other manifestation of the church according to different denominational understandings – which tells them about the nature of Jesus Christ.

Richard has made us more keenly aware of the fellowship of the church, the living communion. Ever since the service of infant dedication, when we were so conscious of the other members of our church joining with us in love, wanting to help rear this child within God's family, we have appreciated their interest and support. We have seen how often Richard's development as a person has moved forward within the context of the church. He loves his church corporately and the members individually, and he associates Jesus closely with the church.

This is true for many other mentally handicapped people in the church environment. It is obvious that their experience of the people who make up the church will colour their picture of the Christ whom they learn about there. If their experience of the church is love, then it is the embodiment of Jesus' love. It will be no good telling them that Jesus loves them if his people are wary and awkward in their company, making them feel isolated or rejected. We are the Body of Christ. It is a solemn lesson, and the significance, highlighted in our dealings with the handicapped, extends far beyond them.

Part of the 'prophetic witness' of handicap may come through the parents and families. Comments from churches asked to reflect on having mentally handicapped people in their midst have included these:

> Having a mentally handicapped child affects your faith in two ways: it challenges and tests your faith, and it greatly strengthens your faith.

> We have all been helped in the church by the courage and faith of the child's parents.

It is easy to get sentimental over this, which is not what most parents want, but it helps to feel something positive can emerge from what often feels a negative, even futile, situation.

Practical jobs

Although people with mental handicaps will usually be slow to learn anything new, many are competent and reliable once they have grasped what is required. They may find it hard to follow verbal instructions, even if they talk fluently and seem to understand what is said to them. Taking in a sequence of 'do this, then do that, then . . .' is difficult. Many work better by eye than ear and find demonstration clearer. It may need a lot of repeating and be full of frustration for teacher and taught before they get it right and can remember what is wanted for another time. The life of the church, however, is full of repeated observances so it may be a good arena in which to practise until they learn.

The ways of our church have been part of Richard's life. We spend more time on the premises than is usual at most

111

churches, because the building is open all day on Sundays, with an open-door policy and meals served. Richard knows the premises inside out, better than most members. He takes his turn as a steward (sidesman) on the chapel door, appearing on the rota one evening a month but functioning more often as he is ever eager to step in, should another steward default for any reason. It took a few weeks for him to manage to collect the offering in a tidy manner, not that easy for it is a large chapel with pillars breaking some rows and the evening congregation is apt to scatter itself widely. Everyone was tolerant of the learning process and eventually he got a flexible system weighed off. Presenting the offering is a matter of great pride and he returns to his place with measured tread. Nowadays a dignified expression has replaced the earlier wide grin of satisfaction as he comes back down the aisle. It is the culmination of his worship. A few minutes later he will be snoring gently through the sermon.

When we move to the hall, he is quickly back in action. He fetches a tray to clear coffee cups, chatting as he does so and keeping a weather-eye open for anything amiss, like a visitor looking lonely, a small child separated from parents in the crowd, or an office door unlocked with possible access to valuables (we are a city centre church!). On the family's monthly turn of duty, he helps prepare and serve lunch. When first allowed in the kitchen, he was not really much help, but he gradually learned. He is still a bit heavy-handed to be put on mass spud-bashing, but he can open tins, count plates into the hot cupboard, and has even made excellent pastry ('tip in two whole bags of flour . . .'). When it came to serving, he began by dishing up vegetables, but that was too much under mother's eye for his liking ('Not so much, it won't go round . . . more than that . . . not on the table!'), so he was glad when promoted to waiter duties. At first he went round the tables in a random manner. Those missed out soon learned to put up their hands for the other waiter to fill in. Keith devised a board game showing the tables, with counters for plates, and made Richard practise a more even distribution until he mastered the idea.

Whether or not it is our turn, Richard always helps clear the tables. Then he moves on to help with teas, provided the week's team welcomes him. He now accepts that some would rather do without his assistance. After the evening service he joins the staff behind the coffee bar, usually handling payments and change, laboriously but with increasing accuracy. He is aware of the whole process, as I have found on the rare occasions I have done the evening refreshments and needed direction.

'I do try to be a useful church member,' he says, and these busy Sundays are the high spot of his week.

We watch him there and reflect on how employable he ought to be – if any employer could bear the first month or so until he learned the ropes!

Our church has been generous and patient towards Richard and in the nature of its ministry there is work for *all* willing hands. The church I first joined as a young teenager, more typically, had less to be done. I remember being eager to do *something* for Christ and the Church but finding not much was wanted. Young people seemed expected to be 'evangelists', and it was hard luck if that was not your gift. How often does the church fail young people when they would like to coin their idealism in service? It is possible that mentally handicapped Christians actually come off better here: churches that welcome them see the need to find them a role.

What can they do? The range reported is wide. Helping with cleaning and catering, moving furniture, gardening, keeping a fresh supply of water in the pulpit carafe, helping with children or with those elderly who are physically disabled, putting up hymn numbers, taking the offering, some even take their turn reading a lesson.

A rural rector with three separate homes for mentally handicapped adults in his parishes describes their contributions:

The young ladies from one home regularly clean the sanctuary at St Michael's and take their turn in doing the offertory procession in the Parish Communion. One takes her turn at reading the lesson. On the first Sunday of December these ladies sang choruses and read a reading, instead of the sermon.

One gentleman from another home is a regular attender at St Michael's and rings the bell for Sunday morning service.

At the next parish one friend from the Home Farm Trust read the third lesson in the Nine Lessons and Carols service before Christmas, and two others take turns to ring the bell for Parish Communion.

I take an interest in all three establishments and they respond. The residents of two of the homes attend church regularly, and I celebrate the Eucharist in one home every Wednesday.

All but three of the Home Farm Trust residents tend to gravitate to the Methodists, but they invite me to lead the carol singing at their Christmas party each year.

If the tasks they can perform are mostly simple and menial, it will be important to recognise that these too are done for Jesus. 'Who sweeps a room as for thy laws makes that and the action fine,' as the hymnwriter George Herbert proclaims. We are not always good at grasping that but, if the basic household chores are neglected, the sanctuary will soon cease to glow to the glory of God. I remember a school visit to a Benedictine monastery, where a monk explained how all shared in the necessary work of the community. The scholarship of the graduate brother would be valued in the proper place, but did not excuse him from taking his turn at cleaning the lavatories. As a schoolgirl I found that a striking point about communal life. As the mother of a handicapped youth, I realise more keenly the need to take life as an integral whole, which should all be offered as a living sacrifice. Some may have very little to offer, but that little is part of the corporate whole.

The widow's mite reminds us of the value of tiny contributions when people give all they can. One church tells of a handicapped youth who had no money and hardly any personal possessions but treasured a pretty painted stone he had been given. One day in his desire to contribute he put his beautiful stone into the plate. Doubtless God saw and appreciated, and so did the church, to have shared the story of his offering.

They may surprise us

Sometimes our handicapped friends may surprise us with what they take on.

I have referred to Richard acting as a steward at church, but this was not something we would have expected him to do. As he grew up we realised that he fancied the job, which he saw his brother doing, but we parents did not see it as appropriate. Regulars might not mind, but we imagined visitors would be put off if greeted at the church door by a Down's youth. However, the church thought otherwise and offered him the chance to try, and now he takes his turn responsibly.

His friendly, direct questions elicit information about newcomers that gets conversation going when he introduces them to someone else. 'This is Peter. He comes from Canada. He's got a wife and two little boys at home.' 'Auntie's friend is here and unhappy. Go and see her.' Thus was I directed to a newly bereaved acquaintance, who could not face her own church that day but was glad of a familiar face.

One week we left Richard helping with teas and went out for an afternoon walk. On our return he was eager to introduce us to Tom and his two friends from the Midlands. Tom had just run the London Marathon. Richard knew about the Marathon from *Blue Peter*, so was suitably impressed. As a result of information he relayed, Richard's father mentioned this to the visiting preacher in the vestry, who in turn expressed a public welcome to the runner (although it was only later that he identified him) and prayed for the work of Tear Fund, on whose behalf Tom had run. As a result the runner received a little extra sponsorship money.

One of the vagrants who come into our hall became noisy one afternoon. A large, middle-aged man, he drinks heavily and can be violent. All had been peaceful when he suddenly got up and began to sing loudly, disturbing everyone. Oh dear, we thought, who is doing to deal with him? No one relishes the task. Suddenly Richard got up and strode purposefully towards him. I was alarmed, but friends made me sit tight and see what would happen. Richard approached the man with an air of authority, took him by the arm and, looking earnestly into his face, told him he must not make such a noise and disturb others in the hall. Pleasantly but firmly Richard escorted him to the door and sent him out. A few minutes later the man reappeared and to our amazement went quietly up to Richard, who was sitting apart with a book, apologised to him for his former behaviour and asked his permission to use the Gents before finally departing!

A retired lady who now often worships at our church is a particular friend of Richard's. Once I thanked her for her kindness to him. 'I suppose you imagine I took the initiative in that,' she said. Then she told me how some years before her sister, a member of the church, had invited Mary to the Harvest Social. They arranged to meet there, but Ruth was badly delayed. Mary hardly knew anyone and sat alone on one side. Richard went up to her and said, in his direct way, 'You look lonely.' 'Yes, I'm waiting for my sister.' 'Who is your sister?' and Richard sat down and chatted to her till Ruth joined them.

Again Richard provides most of my examples because I see what he does, but I have no doubt that other churches have similar experiences.

Churches often mention the ability of many handicapped people to contribute in prayer. 'Can say a prayer, you know,' is the proud claim of at least one man of little speech. The prayers may be short and simple but are often to the point. Addressing God may be easier than speaking to man: they can expect understanding on the part of the Omniscient!

The handicapped may be less prone than many Christians to see religion as a one-day-a-week matter and, being generally less inhibited, they speak more freely of their faith to those outside the church.

One church which runs a club for mentally handicapped adults on Sunday mornings tells how they share in the first part of communal worship and then continue in a separate meeting. This may be held in the church kitchen over coffee, at a local café, or on a bench in the park.

God is everywhere, although you can't see him, and you can talk to him and say a prayer even though you are not in church. If God is the friend who made Coca Cola and flowers and sunshine and is with us all the time and wants us to talk to him, then we say 'Thank you, God' out loud, in the middle of the café, and to the evident embarrassment of those who spend their Sunday mornings differently. And just in case they didn't hear the first time, we shout 'AMEN'. If they don't come to church, we'll take the church to them.

I was surprised when several of our neighbours spoke to me of Richard's baptism. By no means all are churchgoers, but they had all grasped that it was important to Richard, and one wanted to know in detail about Baptist practice. Richard had Good News, so he shared it with all his friends. I could not imagine his articulate parents or brother doing so like that.

Another Down's youth, preparing for believer's baptism, carefully wrote to every member of the staff at his Training Centre, inviting them to the service. Few were Christians, but all were moved to attend.

It is curious that while people in the church still question the rightness of those with severe mental handicaps becoming full, communicant members, others who do not themselves embrace the Christian faith are interested and sympathetic when they hear of handicapped neighbours joining the church.

While we wonder whether they are capable of faith themselves, the handicapped may even be leading others to Christ. One vicar tells of a family sadly torn up by having a Down's child. The sister rejected both the boy and their mother. The mother lost her faith. By the grace of God,

confirmed at the age of thirty-seven, this mentally handicapped man was the means of leading his mother back into the fellowship of the Church and to again receive communion.

The ability to *think* may be limited, but there are mentally handicapped Christians who by their deeds and even by their words are active for Jesus. If we give them the chance, they have a real contribution to make within the church. We might add a further beatitude for them: Blessed are the mentally handicapped, for they shall be known as Friends of Jesus.

Such a one is John. He is twenty-three and, after some years in hospital, lives in a house for mentally handicapped adults run by a Housing Association which originated within a local church. John is just the sort of person you might find sitting in your pew one of these days. A friend from his church tells us about him.

John came from an institutional background but was anxious to find out about life around him in the community. He came to the Baptist church and soon made friends. He joined in the hymns, singing the tunes in a loud voice. His speech was often difficult to understand but John watched and listened and always managed to do the 'right' thing.

Rarely late, although he could not tell the time, John was anxious to become part of the fellowship. He came regularly to the Bible class for mentally handicapped adults which was begun at the church, and was faithful in attendance at worship on Sundays.

He was present at quite a few baptismal services before he said to the minister 'Me next'. This was not put as a question, more as a statement of his faith. There followed discussions by the diaconate and a time when two of the leaders of the mentally handicapped Bible class tried to explain to John the basic truths of the Christian faith, the meaning of baptism, and the responsibilities of church membership. The church members accepted John for baptism and membership.

His baptism was a joyful occasion. Those present will not easily forget John's singing of 'Jesus loves me, this I know' before he was baptised.

His special job has been to help fold some of the church bulletins for Sunday worship, and he has exercised his responsibility as a church member by attending church meetings. 'I must be at the special meeting on Thursday' – and he will be, taking his part as far as possible by listening to those around him and by joining in the worship.

John has much to give. His warm personality and cheerful disposition have endeared him to many. He takes turns to sit with his friends, the people who have welcomed him into the fellowship. He cannot always remember their names but he is

118

concerned if they are missing for a few weeks and will ask for them.

He has enriched the fellowship of our church and for this we thank God.

Notes

2 THE CHALLENGE TO THE CHURCH

1 E.A. Bladon, *Open Wide the Gates*, Diocese of Gloucester, 1986
2 Rodney Clapp, 'Clanking and Humming for Jesus', *Christianity Today*, 13 June 1986
3 International Year of Disabled People Report on Disabled People in Church, 1981
4 Dr Howard Williams, in a sermon on 2 November 1986
5 Joan Bicknell, 'Mentally Handicapped People in the Community: a challenge for the churches', *Crucible*, Oct–Dec 1983
6 Collins, 1987

3 NEW FACES AT CHURCH

1 David G. Wilson, *I Am With You*, St Paul Publications, 1975
2 Bladon, op. cit.
3 Frances Young, *Face to Face*, Epworth Press, 1985
4 Bladon, op. cit.

4 WHAT CAN THE CHURCH DO FOR THEM?

1 Bladon, op. cit.
2 Bladon, op. cit.
3. Wilson, op. cit.
4 Margaret Davies, private publication, 1982

5 CAN THEY LEARN ABOUT JESUS?

1 Universal Declaration of Human Rights, United Nations, 1948, Article 26
2 Bladon, op. cit.
3 Hodder and Stoughton, 1981
4 *Christianity Today*, 13 June 1986, loc. cit.
5 Bladon, op. cit.
6 Davies, op. cit.
7 King's Fund Centre, 126 Albert Street, London NW1 7NF